MEMORIES OF THE ANDES

José Luis 'Coche' Inciarte

Survivor of the 1972 Andes Flight Disaster

First edition published in 2021 by Heddon Publishing.

Spanish language version published by Penguin Random House Grupo Editorial in 2017

Copyright © José Luis Inciarte 2020, all rights reserved.

ISBN 978-1-913166-33-5

Translated from the Spanish version by John Guiver.
Cover design by Catherine Clarke.
Images courtesy of José Luis Inciarte.

www.heddonpublishing.com
www.facebook.com/heddonpublishing
@PublishHeddon

Contents

This memoir is dedicated to my family: my wife, my children and their spouses, and my eight grandchildren whom, so many times in the mountains, I thought I would never have.

No te rindas

No te rindas, por favor no cedas,
aunque el frío queme,
aunque el miedo muerda,
aunque el sol se ponga y se calle el viento,
aún hay fuego en tu alma,
aún hay vida en tus sueños,
porque cada día es un comienzo nuevo,
porque esta es la hora y el mejor momento,
porque no estás sola, porque yo te quiero.

by Mario Benedetti

Don't Give Up

Don't give up, please don't succumb,
even if the cold burns,
even if fear bites,
even if the sun sets and the wind falls silent,
there is still fire in your soul,
there is still life in your dreams,
because every day is a new beginning,
because this is the time and the best moment,
because you are not alone, because I love you.

Prologue

This book is written in memory of my friend Gastón Costemalle.

Dear Gastón

I haven't seen you for forty-eight years. The last time was on 13th October 1972, boarding the plane in Mendoza airport.

Of course, you know what we went through over the following seventy-two days!

So many times, I wanted to be with you in that paradise of peace and happiness; that place where I imagined you to be when I was dying under tons of snow in that infamous avalanche!

From the cold that penetrated my bones, through the most dreadful thirst and the most unimaginable hunger; through anguish and despair and any number of worse feelings; through friends whom I got to know like never before, I became a man.

Continuously undergoing every kind of suffering and humiliation, it is amazing and gratifying to see with how much composure and integrity it is possible to respond!

Experiencing the human warmth that saved us from a frozen death, aware of the importance of another's life for one's own survival, I have also learned, among so many other things, that love between men goes beyond feelings. It is found in human behaviour, which, after that pact in which I was involved, and which I am so proud to have shared in with everyone, allowed us to honour and defend life.

To make the pain more bearable, I searched for meaning and I learned that life is worth living even in the presence of suffering. You and the others who are with you deserved a prize in life, but received death on the mountain, and since then you live on in peace.

I believe that one can find peace in life, and for that you must walk the path of happiness, which must be merited, and then you will need to realize how much more rewarding it is to give than to receive, and that giving has no limit.

Today I am more than seventy years old, and I must be grateful for everything that life has given me. I married, had children, and also enjoy the pleasure of being a grandfather.

To you, dear Gordo, and to all the others who remained with you on the mountain, I want to say that we remember you always and that, with the work of the Fundación Viven, we seek to make a difference. And if, before we meet again, it seems to you that we should be doing something more, then let me know!

To you and the others, my deepest gratitude.

Your friend always

Coche

chapter I Before

From the moment that we found ourselves trapped on the mountain, and even more so once we heard the news on our small salvaged radio that the search had been called off, we didn't have any dream other than to return to everything dear to us; our family, our friends, and the places we loved.

That thought, accompanied by images of my mother, girlfriend, and brother and sisters, was what sustained my spirit in a permanent struggle to stay alive.

But I wasn't alone. God was with me, and my friends who helped me to get through it, whether it was from the living, who were fighting for life just like me, or from the mysterious bond that unites us with the dead.

The project to fulfil that dream had a goal; a common objective: that we should all get out of there alive.

In that attitude, that determination, a superior force was present – a force that I call God (however that may be understood), which was expressed through man and lived in him and for him. Because I saw young boys become men and carry out acts of love, based not just on feelings, but on the manner in which they conducted themselves.

But everything had started much earlier, by which I mean that my previous life, and everything that I had learned in it, were fundamental to my being able to face this enormous challenge which saw me suddenly dropped into such dire circumstances.

I don't know when my family had moved to Punta Gorda, to number 5623 República de Méjico Street. We spent happy years together, living by the sea, opposite the Playa Verde (Green Beach) in Montevideo. We would have improvised games of football with one-metre-wide goals, and kids came from all around the neighbourhood to play. When the beach attendant intervened to stop

Before

the game so that we wouldn't disturb the bathers, he would, if he were a fool, almost always end up in the water; or, if he were a bit wiser, he would head off, quietly whistling, to the other end of the beach where the Yacht Club still is today. Many of my relatives – my Algorta Vazquez aunts and uncles and cousins – lived in the neighbourhood, as did some famous residents such as Leonel Viera, who designed some architectural landmarks in Uruguay, and Eladio Dieste, an engineer and architect who is known throughout the world for his creations.

It was outside this house in República de Méjico Street, that my girlfriend Soledad stopped by to pick me up on 12th October 1972, to drive me to Carrasco airport. She came in the Beetle with Gastón Costemalle Jardí and Pancho Delgado, whom she had picked up in Pocitos, another beach-side neighbourhood.

They studied law and agronomy, but Gastón was my friend from the Windsor School kindergarten. Years later, he had changed to Stella Maris College, run by the Christian Brothers, while I continued at the English college. Pancho had completed his primary and secondary education at the Jesuit 'Seminary' College.

I think I was the only one who had completed all stages of my education at a secular English college, where we played football rather than rugby.

I had never played rugby, and I didn't understand why it was played with an oval ball that might bounce in any direction, and why you had to be running forward when the ball was passed back. In addition, they would tackle each other as if they were doing battle, and would applaud when the ball was kicked out!

Football is still my passion, and in my country, I am a 'bolsilludo' fan, as they call the supporters of the Club Nacional de football, the doyen of Uruguayan football; the club that developed, among many other crack players, Luis Suárez.

But yes, it's true that the majority of those who were travelling on the plane were rugby players and alumni of Stella Maris College, including Tintín Vizintín, Roberto Canessa, and Nando Parrado; the three who left on the final expedition, when after two months of desperate survival, all that remained for us was to walk into the unknown, in search of help which might be many miles away from the inhospitable environment into which we had fallen.

At my school, which was at first called Windsor School and went on to become the Ivy Thomas Memorial School, I was part of the inaugural high school class. I had some male classmates, but the vast majority were female. For various reasons, by the time I finished the fourth year of high school, I was the only remaining male, which explains why my friends at that time were almost all former students of Stella Maris and of the Old Christians.

Memories of the Andes

The English school was secular, but had, as its main standard, the great humanist values that the poet Rudyard Kipling captured in his poem *If*.

If you can keep your head when all about you
Are losing theirs and blaming it on you,
If you can trust yourself when all men doubt you,
But make allowance for their doubting too;
If you can wait and not be tired by waiting,
Or being lied about, don't deal in lies,
Or being hated, don't give way to hating,
And yet don't look too good, nor talk too wise:

If you can dream – and not make dreams your master;
If you can think – and not make thoughts your aim;
If you can meet with Triumph and Disaster
And treat those two impostors just the same;
If you can bear to hear the truth you've spoken
Twisted by knaves to make a trap for fools,
Or watch the things you gave your life to, broken,
And stoop and build 'em up with worn-out tools:

If you can make one heap of all your winnings
And risk it on one turn of pitch-and-toss,
And lose, and start again at your beginnings
And never breathe a word about your loss;
If you can force your heart and nerve and sinew
To serve your turn long after they are gone,
And so hold on when there is nothing in you
Except the Will which says to them: 'Hold on!'

If you can talk with crowds and keep your virtue,
Or walk with Kings nor lose the common touch,
If neither foes nor loving friends can hurt you,
If all men count with you, but none too much;
If you can fill the unforgiving minute
With sixty seconds' worth of distance run,
Yours is the Earth and everything that's in it,
And – which is more – you'll be a Man, my son!

Eternal Peaks (Cover art)

I call this painting Eternal Peaks.

It is simply the cordillera, where I bring into play the forms and the rhythms.

I've seen it hundreds of times from the air, and always I seem to see the Valley of Tears, where the accident occurred; that horseshoe-shaped valley that seems to recur constantly, and the overall appearance of the mountain is achieved by the replication of this shape. This is as seen from the air, because I suspect that Nando and Roberto, who crossed it on foot in the final expedition, would not agree that it recurs.

It looks majestic and immense, and I remember that I was held captive there; that I lived seventy-two days on it, and I can't quite believe it. Sometimes it seems to be more fiction than fact!

I think that the values so well expressed by Kipling in *If* harmonize perfectly with the religion of the Irish Brothers of Stella Maris and the Jesuits of the Seminary, so I believe that, in effect, both my friends and I had a very similar education. I was, and I am, Catholic.

When the Dalai Lama was asked "What is the best religion?" his response was: "The one that makes you a better person" – with which I am in complete agreement.

This communion of ideals and values was an important element that allowed us to manage the calamitous situation of having to live in the mountains. In addition, I am convinced that the story of the Andes and the values that derive from it don't preclude any religion, race, social class, or sport. They are the heritage of all men.

That 12ᵗʰ October 1972, as Soledad drove the Beetle across Carrasco Bridge, heading towards the airport, I gave my customary greeting to the district of Canelones which we were entering, and I said goodbye to Montevideo until the following Sunday. It would be only four days.

The greeting was from an old custom that my father had taught me: to greet and give thanks to the districts that make up our country.

We arrived at the airport happy, and we were happy when boarding the Uruguayan Air Force plane. Never again in my life have I flown with passengers who were in such high spirits! We didn't know everyone, but that day it was as if a previous strong bond united us. The joy was the common denominator in that plane; a joy that didn't diminish despite the setback of having to spend a night in Mendoza, Argentina, because of bad weather that would have made crossing the Andes very dangerous.

I remember how Gastón Costemalle was enjoying jumping on the beds of the guesthouse where we stayed overnight, until he fell to the floor when one of them gave way and split down the middle.

The next day, we left quietly to take the bus to El Plumerillo airport. It was the morning of Friday 13ᵗʰ October 1972, the day on which I saw my dear friend Gastón Costemalle for the last time.

My Father

My father was the third of four children born to Nicolás Inciarte Caminos and Manuela Imenarrieta Mujica, making me a distant relative of the former President of Uruguay, Pepe Mujica.

Before

Nicolás was the first Inciarte to arrive in Uruguay, and he did so in the 19th century, along with his widowed mother. He carried out various activities as a farm worker, helping with the livestock and in the warehouse. He was a very intelligent and tireless worker. Later, he married Manuela and had four children: Alfredo (lawyer), Adolfo (civil engineer), Ricardo, my father (agronomist), and Sofia.

My father was studying medicine, and was already well-advanced in that career when a medical condition caused him to change to agronomy – he had contracted tuberculosis and needed to be in a clean-air environment. He already had somewhere to go, since my grandfather Nicolás at his death, on 22nd December 1928, had left a farm as well as some other properties. An entire fortune accomplished in a short time! But, due to the bad administration of some of my grandfather's heirs, the huge extent of lands that he once owned has been drastically reduced, leaving just 700 hectares, on which there is a dairy farm. This is the farm on which my father began his dairy work; a field in which he became a pioneer and national authority.

He had started as an employee, working as a dairy inspector, and then later his duties expanded when, in 1936, the producers group initially known as Cole became Conaprole, the cooperative of which my father was the technical industrial manager until the day of his death, on 27th December 1966.

The plaque that his Conaprole colleagues put on his grave is a faithful reflection of him as a person. "Exemplary friend, loyal collaborator, exceptional technician, and driving force of the Uruguayan dairy industry".

The main Conaprole production facility, located to the north of the city of Florida, was named the Ricardo R. Inciarte Plant in his honour.

I was just eighteen years old when my father died. Ever since, it has left a vacuum in my life that has been impossible to fill – by his absence; by the want of his joy and his advice; because he was my father and my friend; because I no longer have someone with whom to share my happiest or most difficult moments.

I remember that almost every weekend I would head out to the farm with him. I loved to accompany him to a place that we both liked equally.

The trip took hours, as he first used to stop at the Vidiella winery, over in Peñarol on the outskirts of Montevideo, to pick up a box of red wine and to chat with his colleague, Mr Vidiella.

After passing through La Paz, Las Piedras, and Progreso, we would arrive at Canelones, where there was a Conaprole plant that produced seventy-kilogram wheels of Gruyère cheese. My father would hoist a half-wheel of the cheese into the back of the Dodge truck, to enjoy later, accompanied by the red wine.

The hours would pass and, arriving at a crossroad, we would turn towards the town of Santa Lucia, where we would have lunch in the restaurant at the Biltmore Hotel – all without any rush, progressing at the leisurely speed of the Dodge, which couldn't go any faster than sixty kilometres an hour.

Later, we would drive across the old iron bridge at the Pache crossing of the Santa Lucia River. We would give our greetings to the Florida district and bid farewell to Canelones. Later still, we would go past the small Florida Conaprole plant, which was a sheet-metal storehouse that received the dairy production from the surrounding area, and sometimes we would also stop there. These days, my father's name gleams on the front of that same building, which is now Powdered Milk Production Facility Number 7.

At that point, the dilapidated tarmac road ended and the gravel section of Route 5 began. We went through La Cruz, Pintado, and Sarandí Grande, and after Puntas de Maciel we finally reached kilometre 162, which marked the entrance to our premises. Today, the entrance is at kilometre 156.5, as the new layout of Route 5 is more direct than before.

Once we were in our country house, the moment came to taste the wine and the delicious Gruyère, followed by a dinner after which we would go to bed.

In the early morning, we would go out riding around the countryside on horseback and not return until noon, when the traditional pre-lunch aperitif would begin once again.

On the premises, there was already a functioning dairy farm and I don't remember how many cows were hand-milked by the light of several kerosene lamps.

The nearest dairy farm in the vicinity was quite a distance away, on the outskirts of Florida, the capital city of the district of that name. There were several other dairies in the villages but each only provided for the local community.

At that time, my father already did the dairy control for Conaprole, weighing the monthly yield per milking for each cow, which made it possible to track each animal throughout the year and to identify the most productive ones. That was the only way to achieve genetic improvement back then, at a time when the cows were known by name rather than a number on an ear tag. The milk destined for the cities and the capital underwent pasteurization and quality control, which was not the case in the villages, where water of dubious origin used to be added to the milk.

Before

Many's the time that I witnessed a rusty old tin, that had once held peaches in syrup, being used to add water from the rain gutter to the thirty-litre milk churns, which were then picked up for distribution by a horse-drawn carriage.

It was on these trips that I learned so much from my father, from his life, from his intelligent conversations, deep but at the same time funny, their advice remaining with me to the present day. And I still carry everything deep inside me, but so many years have already passed.

"Here there was nothing," he would say to me, pointing out the facilities and hundreds of Holstein cattle. He would say it proudly, and with good reason! I was happy to accompany him and to listen to him very attentively. He had the gift of teaching, which he put to good use in the Dairy Department of the Faculty of Agronomy.

My life had been easy up until the day on which, when I was at a birthday party very close to my house, my twelve-year-old sister turned up to let me know that our father had suffered a heart attack. I left for home with her immediately, along with my cousin Beto, Gastón Costemalle, my girlfriend Soledad, and some other friends.

I arrived to a terrible scene that I will never forget, which I think was the most shocking and painful of my life: my father lying in bed, and my Uncle Roberto striving to compress his chest while my grandfather gave him artificial respiration. I approached him instinctively as if I would like to help, my gaze fixed on his chest, which was going up and down as though he were really breathing. At one point, I turned to my mother, who never took her eyes off Dad, her face soaked in tears. His chest went up and down, until my grandfather said, "It's enough" and fell, exhausted, crying over this body immobilized by death.

I looked again at my mother, who was crying inconsolably at the loss of the husband she loved. To see her grieve over her loss at that moment overcame even the enormous grief I was experiencing myself. I went to her and we hugged one another, stricken by a suffering that I can't describe.

From that moment, I decided to in some way fill the gap that my father had left – to do all within my reach to fulfil the role of head and protector of the family.

I thought about how I would take care of my mother, who otherwise would not stop mourning her husband. And my sisters and brother, who also were mourning their father – I intended to take care of them as well. And those concerns prevented me from grieving quite so much. I was looking at my mother, at my sisters, and at my brother, and I realized that a man must do what's appropriate when the circumstances call for it. And to this day I've taken care of everything that I could.

Punta Gorda

I painted this at the request of my sister, Marta; who, like me, or perhaps even more so, yearns for the time when we lived with our parents. It was the summer home of my maternal grandparents, Alberto Vázquez Barriere and Mary Callander. They had loaned it to their eldest daughter, my mother, and to my father, whom I suspect my grandparents adored.

It was here that I lived with my family: my father, mother, and brother and sisters. It was here that my life was spent as a student, when I loved to accompany my father to the countryside. Until, abruptly, everything ended. A black abyss opened in front of me when my father died.

I did not fall into that abyss; instead, and even to my own amazement, I decided to take care of everything he had built up. I decided it with a cold mind, rather than crying and feeling sorry for myself. He was already buried, and I had to look to the future and see what to do in this new situation. Therefore, this figurative painting is of the house where I was happy with the love and protection of my parents.

When I married Soledad, I continued living in that house, and so it was that she, my great love, took care of me, as she is doing still. I haven't had much time to attend to my father. I regularly visit the cemetery where I left him on 27th December 1966 – and I talk to him. Also, every time that I pass the gate of the Buceo cemetery, I still say, fifty years later, "Dad, I love you, and I miss you very much." I would very much like to see him again.

Before

I was in charge of the funeral. I think that it was my uncle Algorta who helped me with the formalities. For a long time he had a fatherly attitude towards me, and we did the things that we had to do.

I remember that at the cemetery a Conaprole director made a speech highlighting the great work accomplished by my father.

To this day, I often go to the cemetery to visit him at his final resting place. I go to speak with him, especially at those moments when I want some reference and I need his support, in my joys as much as in my difficulties. It gives me a lot of peace, and I always return with an answer. It's incredible but that's how it is. The old man is still helping me just as he always did during his life.

Since 2008, my mother has also been there with him.

Soledad

When she was twenty-nine, Soledad wrote this account of her memories of taking us to the airport.

I started going out with Coche when I was seventeen. Before that, we had been great friends. He would always tell me many things and we laughed a lot together. I felt very good being with him. He was extremely caring, a lot of fun, very happy, and had something immensely warm in his eyes.

Then one day something changed; our mundane and simple conversations became profound and difficult, we began to feel more awkward, our glances met... and we gazed into each others eyes for the first time... We had fallen in love, almost without realizing it.

From then on I was immensely happy; as happy as one can be at age seventeen, in that magical world of romance, of hopes and dreams. Our lives were taken up with planning and dreaming of the future, forgetting that most of the time it is uncertain, and situations don't always turn out as we might imagine them. Certainly, like everyone else in the world, I had some frustrations and disappointments, which left their trace to some extent but which were almost never related to him, and moreover any small complications that did arise would always be resolved. At the time, I felt safe, and capable of facing whatever came my way and adapting it to my advantage. I walked through the world with a firm step, and in general, I had no fear of anything. My attitude was defiant and although I realized that at some point life might provide my share of suffering, such a thing seemed distant and detached...

Memories of the Andes

On Wednesday 11th October 1972, I returned from work, as on every other day. I was twenty-two years old, and a secretary at my father's law firm. Coche had headed out to the farm to leave everything in order before his trip to Chile. He had been invited on that trip by Gastón Costemalle, his great friend, to fill up the charter flight, and to spend the weekend together.

Since the death of his father in 1966, Coche had been working on his family's farm; a dairy establishment with some agriculture and some sheep. He had only a few courses left to complete his agronomy degree. That day, after sorting everything out, he planted a tree, a carob, in what was going to be the garden of our future home. The old house of his parents and grandparents had been torn down years previously, and we planned to live in a chalet which had been built in its place and to which we were planning to make some minor alterations. All this was already underway because our wedding day was only a few months away.

The garden was practically non-existent; it was an area of open field separated by a wire fence from the rest of the field where some animals grazed. Two silver poplars grew opposite where our bedroom was going to be, but they were still very small. At that time, we were dreaming of a lovely park, with many trees that would fill our lives with their different shades of green, and their thousand glimmers of shadow and light.

At 7:00 p.m. Coche returned to Montevideo, and came to see me. The next day he would be flying to Chile.

On Thursday 12th October I woke up very early. As I lived in the neighbourhood of Pocitos, I was first going to pick up Pancho Delgado, then Gastón Costemalle, and finally Coche, who lived in Punta Gorda, all on the way to the airport. I had ended up taking them in my parents' car, which enabled me to see them off. It was a clear sunny day, with only a few clouds appearing to the west.

We reached the airport with time to spare. It was full of the boys and their families who were there to see them off. The purpose of the trip was a friendly game of rugby. But several other boys made up the passenger numbers without being part of the team. Coche was one of those. This team was composed of former students of the Stella Maris College (The Old Christians), and those who were with them were all friends or acquaintances of the players. So we knew almost everyone who had gone there to see them off. The joy was all around for everyone to see.

At 9:05 a.m., the first passenger call could be heard over the PA system: "TAMU announces flight 571 to Santiago in Chile." My heart tightened slightly. Farewells have always made me emotional, even with the prospect of a quick return. I find it very difficult

Before

to separate from someone I love, and who in one way or another is present in my life. It is difficult to cope with their absence, with the inability to participate from afar, and with imagining what they are doing each day. It is difficult to get used to breaking my dependence on them, to the fact that they in their absence are not depending on me; and to the alteration of the rhythm that marks their presence in my waking hours. It is especially difficult when that someone has become the cornerstone of my life.

The habitual closeness of those that we love is so strong, so ingrained, that their absence always produces a void. A void that we fill, or try to fill, with a thousand and one important or superfluous activities, so that this empty space stays unnoticed, and we are not overcome by melancholy. But on occasion we like to immerse ourselves in it.

The PA system repeated the boarding call. The time had come. We all began to say our goodbyes. We hugged... we smiled at each other, we hugged again. I put a chocolate in his pocket, but he didn't notice. We walked together in an embrace for a few seconds, rapidly whispering to each other everything that we wouldn't be able to say over the next few days. We were already at the boarding area. A last kiss, a last embrace. His thinking already directed towards his documents and his journey, mine towards my solitude. And from further away, a wink, and, in me, a tear, a hidden tear.

I went running up the stairs that led to the observation terrace. The runway shimmered under the rays of the sun. The plane was there, not very large, white with a grey belly and black nose. Unlike other aircraft, its wings were above the fuselage. I leant against the railing, next to Daniel Juan, president of the Old Christians.

"What type of plane is it?"

"A Fairchild," he told me.

I took note of the letters on the plane. I did so subconsciously, while waiting for the boys to appear on the tarmac. In big black letters 'Fuerza Aérea Uruguaya' and the number '571'. Something caused me to remember it.

The boys spilled out onto the tarmac. Everyone looked up and waved to where we were on the balcony. Coche among them, smiling at me. I also smiled at him; the narrow aircraft ladder, the last step, the threshold... his eyes on mine for the last time; his smile and his goodbye also for the last time... Already everything separates us, and how much more would separate us...

Today I have this image rooted in my memory; I have never been able to forget it among the images of my life; it will always occupy a prominent place. For a long time that last smile would be my pillar. For a long time that goodbye would be his final gift...

Memories of the Andes

The noise of the engines interrupted our farewells; the white bird began to soar, all-powerful and defiant in the vast blue expanse. Human ingenuity conquering nature once more.

I returned via the Rambla without any problem. The October sun was already starting to heat up. And then on the horizon, I caught sight of dark clouds to the west. A small foreboding that I wanted to dismiss.

On that first day of his absence, I tried, as always, to follow my normal routine, but my concentration was constantly being interrupted by the wandering of my thoughts.

He had gone, but he remained in me. I was here, but I had gone in him.

How important is the living of one in another!

How important are the thoughts and actions that we motivate in one another! It is enough that we want it so.

My thoughts continued their course, stopping every hour, trying to locate him in time and space. I made a thousand and one journeys, I imagined a thousand and one situations; I recalled moments we had experienced, and invented new ones.

How vast and wide is the mind's world, how unlimited! There everything is possible without too much effort.

"It is necessary in life to make allowances for chance. Chance, ultimately, is God." (Anatole France)

13th October 1972 branded my life forever.

When I got up and went out that next day I couldn't even have imagined the events that would be unleashed in a few hours' time.

A phone call from my friend Rosina ... in a choked voice she tried to tell me the news. That call, suddenly and at point-blank range, darkened the happy and carefree existence that I'd experienced until then. I couldn't imagine how much more painful and distressing it was going to be to deal with what was to come.

"The aircraft is lost, it hasn't arrived at its destination." How to assimilate those words? How to understand them? How to stay standing when the pain is so great that it drowns, suffocates, rips one apart?

When that anguish takes away your breath, when fear paralyzes everything vital within you.

Before

On that day, I knew what it was to feel that pain, that anguish, and that fear for the first time.

None of them can be explained with words. One only knows them by experiencing them, and that knowledge, I reiterate, drowns, suffocates and tears you apart.

Those happy young men, the festivity at the airport, the last smile on the aircraft ladder, are all gone... they are already a memory.

Taking Charge

Life before my father died was very different to how it was afterwards. Back then my father and my mother took care of my brother and sisters and me. I was mainly occupied with my studies, and I also used to accompany my father to the farm. Sometimes my grandfather would make the house at Punta del Este available and we would go there for a few days. We would go and pick up some Argentinian cousins, who were quite a bit older than me, and with them riding in the back of our Dodge truck we would head off to eat at Mariskonea; a traditional restaurant on the peninsula. My father also liked to go and have a drink with his old friends in a place called My Drink, near where the Brava Beach began, and he would invite me along.

The friends requested their cocktails or whiskeys and just when I was about to ask for a Coke, I heard them say, "An Alexander for him": a drink that had cream and was smoother. So from then on, just as I would drink wine when I was at the Vidiella winery, I would drink an Alexander in My Drink. Those are a few fond memories of my life back then.

When he died, I took charge. And I think that for many years I succeeded in doing it, albeit with stumbling and difficulties.

I had taken care of everything, in addition to which I was studying, and working on the farm. But six years on, I found myself able to take advantage of there being no classes at the college – due to a strike – to spend a long weekend in Chile, and so have the opportunity to see the effects of Salvador Allende's government in a country in which the peso was worth almost nothing against the dollar. We knew that there were all sorts of shortages, and so we brought along cigarettes, which, after the accident, served us very well on the mountain.

I had already gone to Chile the previous year with my cousin Beto, in a Citroën 2CV pick-up, and it had gone very well. The country had been in the middle of an electoral campaign for some elections that Dr Salvador Allende had ended up winning.

The Fairchild

But when we plunged into the mountains, my life changed once again. Just as when my father died I had lost the previous life in which my parents had taken care of me, when I fell into the Andes I lost the previous life in which I took care of my family. And I thought that from there on in, I needed to take care of this new family; this society of the snow that was forming.

And I swear that I did as much as possible, despite the tiredness, despite the feeble effort of my lungs, and despite legs which felt like lead.

I took care of what I could: I was attentive in consoling someone who was crying, or who was prey to a sudden imbalance. I would try to help if I realized that someone had become depressed.

Even though our condition was hopeless, a small caring gesture was always possible, and I tried to provide it. The task that I started, to try to control the anxiety that was always threatening to invade us, was far from easy. Because everything was a struggle up there. I'm not referring to problems amongst ourselves, which, even though they occurred, were small and infrequent, but to the permanent struggle against nature, the struggle to stay alive, to not let yourself succumb to death, and it is that same will to struggle that allows you to continue living. And that struggle doesn't allow you a moment of peace.

Before

What would become of my family without me? A desperate need to know the answer overwhelmed me in those crazy seconds when the Fairchild was careering down the mountain, moments after its wing had crashed against one of the peaks.

That crash signified a profound break; both in the plane, which literally split in two, and in my life, where I entered a period of maturation and deep discovery of human nature. In the same way that I had taken responsibility to look after my family from age eighteen, I tried as much as possible, after the accident, to take care of my companions who, like me, had been left totally helpless in the most inhospitable surroundings that you could imagine. I did as I was able in response to the different circumstances that took place during those seventy-two days which, although very painful and uncertain, were also a time of great learning.

chapter II The first sixteen days

To begin with, there was a party atmosphere inside the plane. We were constantly going from one side of the plane to the other, and we were making and playing joke upon joke. But a first air pocket accomplished what the repeated urgings of crew had failed to do: to get us all to sit down and fasten our seatbelts.

A second air pocket, deeper than the first, made me think that there might be problems. We heard "give me power" from the cockpit, followed by the sound of the engines revving up to their maximum power. The cabin inclined steeply as the aircraft attempted to climb, pressing my body back against my seat. Everything was vibrating! Nothing was visible through the windows – only the white clouds.

In the middle of that terrible vibration, over the noise of the engines straining at full power, we suddenly heard a loud explosion. We had crashed against a mountain in the middle of the Andes! I was conscious of this, but I didn't have time to process it.

Immediately, the roar of engines ceased and the cabin stopped vibrating. Only something like a whistling and a rush of air indicated that the aircraft had split open or fractured somewhere. With my eyes shut tight, I then felt a big impact or belly flop, and the impression that we were sliding rapidly down the mountain.

Air, snow and fuel were pounding my body, which was crouched down in response to the impact, as I was grasping the seat in front.

I always wondered what I would have seen if I hadn't closed my eyes at that point. What was it that came so close as to leave my tie completely in shreds below the knot?

I was expecting to crash against one of those many black rocks that I had seen emerging from the snow. I was twenty-four years old and in fear of dying in the next few seconds!

I see it all clearly. The only time I close my eyes is when I feel the impact. I think that moments before, when we were all being pressed back by the inclination of the aircraft, Pancho and I glanced at each other. The engines are making some brutal noises, and I think, 'Shit, it might crash.' And suddenly, when I feel the explosion, I close my eyes.

'Fuck, it has crashed.' And then, when the engines are no longer making any noise, I say to myself, 'This plane is flying on nothing. And the air and even the snow are coming in – we're done for!'

From that point on, my eyes stay closed, and I'm holding on to the seat-back in front, head between my legs. Until it stops abruptly and because of the brutal impact everything is ripped out from its place and crashes to the front. And afterwards we find out that some have been killed by this accumulation of objects and seats thrown forward by the violence of the collision. But the place where I'm sitting doesn't suffer any impact, because there is nothing behind me. I'd had no idea that there was nothing behind me! It had all disappeared. I realize it once we have stopped, and I look to escape, to flee, coward that I was!

I didn't want to see or hear, I just wanted to leave. That was my first impulse, my first instinct, to distance myself from the situation. But then I said to myself, 'You can't run away from this, it has already happened and now we must deal with it, and we'll figure out how...'

I must be truthful – when the plane stopped, I wanted to remove myself from everything that I saw and heard.

Looking to the back, I couldn't believe that half of the plane, where my friends had been sitting, was missing. Gastón was no longer there! Nor anyone or anything behind me – I was the last. Silence reigned.

Absolute silence. Then, as if someone was switching up the volume, the groans, cries, screams, requests for relief started, and the recurrent "What happened?"

The most astonishing thing was that I was alive, and that there were many more who were alive and unharmed like me.

You feel that life ceases to be that law that makes you master of the world, and becomes something different, something that one must merit!

There was no space and no time to mourn, or cry, or even to suffer a little. We had to act, to manage the chaos; it was vital to bring order to it. No one ran off hysterically, distancing themselves from that sudden horror. Everyone went to the aid of the wounded, who were crying out desperately for relief. And so our space and time were occupied by taking care of them, and that's how it all started!

Those recent days of happiness, of joy, of work and study, were now far away in the distance, but we had little time to contemplate that because the present demanded action. Everything had changed and everything had been lost; nothing from our past survived there. With deep sadness and torn by the pain, I understood that for those who were alive, another life had just begun.

So many alive and unharmed? What was going on?

Faith Moves Mountains

This depicts the mountain that was our home for seventy-two days.

Towards the bottom of the drawing there is a body with its arm lying flat against its side, looking like the long ridge of a mountain. Perhaps the one crowned with the tomb of our friends who died on the mountain, and represented by a body lying face-down.

Above the body you can see an upturned hand; the hand that guided us, that appeared when we most needed it, and that never grew weary.

Further above, other hands open up the mountain; the hands of faith. Beyond that, the eyes of the body to whom those hands belong, and who observed our behaviour and our attitude towards that life that we had to live.

Chaos (Drawing)

This is the first thing I saw when I raised my head from between my legs, once the severed plane had abruptly stopped its slide through the snow, downhill from the point of impact.

Chaos (Painting)

This is an oil painting, made after 2002, the year I started painting in the studio of Sergio Viera (Cruz del Sur).

Memories of the Andes

I had done the first drawing in 1972. It shows the moment at which the broken fuselage came to an abrupt halt, having crashed against the mountain, and having careered downhill through the snow. But that drawing was slightly different from the later painting. Against the walls there were only seats, bodies entangled with each other, scattered shoes, some odd pieces of clothing, and faces that seemed to be screaming and pleading for help. Those screams were the ones that broke the silence after the plane stopped. Also, I had drawn Fito, with his face swollen, asking me "What happened?" and myself, observing everything, uninjured and completely conscious of what had happened. Stunned and shocked by this turn of events, but mostly amazed that I was alive!

The painting Chaos derives from the earlier drawing, but I also pour into it things that happened during the seventy-two days. Dismembered and torn bodies... the colour red everywhere, from the blood that our bodies shed and from the bodily disarray, which we could never put in order; but which I tried to synthesize and give order to in this painting with shapes and rhythms.

Also, you can see the snow through the oval windows, and through the cockpit windshield that traps the pilots.

Above, in the centre, in red, is the Exit sign which could be seen all night. It was so ironic! How could we get out of there?

Many of those who appear here are the sons or brothers of those who were rewarded with the joy of reunion. Others were not. To them is directed my eternal gratitude. They are in the grave, but for me they never died, because I never forget them, and they are in me forever. In human existence, one shares life, and then death.

The first sixteen days

The horizon, which from my home in Punta Gorda appeared far away across the sea, was now close by, high and overwhelming, impossible to avoid – the mountain had us trapped!

The floor of the fuselage extended beyond the end of the broken walls of the aircraft, jutting out a few metres. I crossed the frame that formed the edge of where the plane had split and went out onto a sort of terrace suspended above the snow. There were others there who seemed to be in the same state as me, still not having fully processed what had happened.

The only thing that could be seen was an expanse of snow, punctuated by some black rocks, and the unmistakeable track left by the fuselage in its mad rush down the mountain. And all across that desolate landscape, it was snowing.

Someone was stumbling towards us along the fuselage track. We shouted to him, but he disappeared as if the snow had swallowed him. Some of us jumped out to try to help him, but as soon as we hit the snow we sank to our waists.

It wasn't possible to escape, it wasn't possible to hide the new and shocking reality, and it wasn't possible to stop hearing the injured. It wasn't possible, even, to be a bit cowardly.

We had to stop complaining and to start acting as soon as possible.

I only had a single wound, shaped like a '7', on my knee. It would have hurt me more if I had fallen off a bicycle. And yet look at that disaster that I drew, and it was all silence, and I couldn't believe it. I was dressed in a shirt, trousers, and nylon socks, but not shoes, which had fallen off.

And if you threw yourself onto the snow to escape, it was impossible, because you would sink to the waist. It seems to me that I did throw myself, because I remember the terror of sinking deeper and deeper.

It wasn't possible to escape, nor to cover one's ears. And that was when this nineteen-year-old kid said, "Hey guys, let's stop complaining, and go to help the injured, can't you hear their cries?"

On seeing this kid act, I said to myself, 'This is logical, it's what we must do.'

Memories of the Andes

Let's stop feeling sorry for ourselves, we've already crashed, it's already happened! We can't rewind back to the beginning; we can only act forward from now on. And you hear the boys scream and you say, "Let's go." And you see a tube removed from Enrique Platero's belly and Alvarito's leg get fixed up, and you see the kid and Gustavo Zerbino and Roy Harley working ceaselessly, going to and fro, attending to one person after another.

And so we continue until nightfall, almost a betrayal, and with it, the cold, the new cold that aches and hurts. Everyone more or less dressed the same, with trousers and shirt, moccasins and nylon socks, nothing more.

It was a sort of relief in a way when the night-time fell, because you could no longer see anything. You didn't have to cover your eyes. But your hearing got sharper in the silence of the night. The darkness was impenetrable and your eyes couldn't get used to it. You saw nothing, you were walking and stepping on everyone.

Suddenly, I see some netting hooked to the roof of the fuselage and I climb in, looking for a refuge where I can rest, close my eyes and forget about the disaster for a moment, and almost immediately someone else climbs in and I tell him "I'm here," but on the other hand I felt the heat of his body and he must have felt mine. "Hey man, turn around as my back's freezing." And then he turns around, and later: "Don't let me go to sleep because we'll freeze." And we say to each other, "If I sleep hit me," or "If I go very quiet it's because I've fallen asleep, so wake me up." And so we spend the night talking.

When I saw him, I thought, "Sonofabitch! That's the kid who was doing everything yesterday!" And we spent the night in each other's arms, we gave each other warmth, we saved each other.

I slept with him that night, but I didn't know who it was. The next morning when I woke, I knew his name because we'd already been introduced. We had slept in the hammock formed by the netting that had secured the baggage, although to say 'sleep' is overstating it because we spent the night trying only to survive. In the night when we were 'sleeping', he had asked "What's your name?"

"Coche," I said.

"Corcho?" he asked.

The first sixteen days

"No, you idiot! Coche!" and already I was starting to warm up. My nerves had become fully active, tingling across my whole body.

In all, out of the twenty-seven who were still alive, twenty-four were unharmed. It's a miracle, that, because we should all have been dead! That's what logic dictated, that's what they thought in Montevideo. But logic was a word without meaning up there.

And that's how it was. Everyone who was fit and able went around giving help to those who needed it, with just our hands to give a caress and our words to offer comfort.

The fact of our being alive was triumphing over the prison to which we'd begun to adapt. Life was showing itself to be above all the suffering; it had to bear it, yes, but it seemed worthy of being lived.

"Coche, not Corcho." We experienced cold as if we were going to die. It was a never-ending night, the hands of time had frozen, just like us.

A dark night, impenetrable and dense, to which your eyes couldn't adapt. We didn't see the reality but we could hear the moans of our friends. I had survived the crash, but I would surely die from that cold that paralyzed you if you stayed still. It immobilized you, and it was like an anticipation of death.

To get to my sleeping place, I had stumbled over people who cried out, and over others who no longer did, and, in the embrace of a living body, I spent the longest night of my life. I thought that I would never see a new dawn. But with the passing of the hours, which also seemed frozen by the cold, a new day eventually began to shed its light through the oval windows. It was Saturday, 14th October.

And the sun rose. That sunrise was rather unbelievable. And the fact that, by the grace of God, I was still alive was even more of a shock than the whole disaster.

Still alive! Embracing another who had given me his warmth, and to whom I had given mine. The warmth of the human body saved us that first night. Until then, I didn't know the importance of that discovery: the relevance of another's life for one's own survival! We would have to take care of each other to keep living. We couldn't do it alone. And this was a constant in every subsequent day.

That kid, who had given me warmth that first night, was the first to stop complaining, and he began to act immediately. He attended to the wounded, he organized the chaos in which we found ourselves, and I was impressed by his capacity to serve. All of us who were healthy followed his lead. I admired this proactive and bold teenager who was constantly moving, helping those in need, particularly the wounded.

As soon as the first light of day appeared, I recognized my night-time companion – it was the young man I had admired so much. His name was Roberto Canessa, he was nineteen years old and an undergraduate medical student. From then on he was… and still is… Dr Canessa. He was the person with the most authority…

You could see clearly now, and already many of the cries had died down. I thought that they were sleeping, but some had now died. Then we went out, walking between the living and the dead, to see what it was like outside.

It was a beautiful day. On exiting, we saw the full extent of the disaster. I wasn't tempted to throw myself into the snow and sink to my waist – I had already tried that.

We were trying to make an inventory of who was missing and of who we all were. And Roberto said, "We are going to take out the dead because it's not possible to sleep and there's not enough room here for everyone." I came out to reproach him, "Hey, can you try to be a bit more sensitive?" "Why don't you go fuck yourself?" he replied. Insufferable brat!

We had had to build a wall immediately, with suitcases and whatever else we could find, at the point where the plane had split, so as to stop the cold from coming in, because otherwise we would have frozen. I think it was the team captain who assured us: "Someone will know what happened and will come looking for us," and that gave us peace of mind during those first days after the accident.

We had to consider the extreme urgency of organizing the chaos we found ourselves in. That was necessary, and even more so at the beginning, before a new and unknown situation would arise, which would take us to a more basic primitivism than I imagine man ever experienced.

Our lives had changed in minutes and we couldn't believe what our eyes saw. But nothing would be as before, it could not be worse.

The first sixteen days

We organized what we could, always expecting that they would come to rescue us at any moment, because we were proceeding on the assumption that someone would already know what had happened to our flight and where to find us.

Marcelo Perez del Castillo, the captain of the rugby team, was the person who led that first attempt to adapt to our situation. He was the leader that everyone followed, and he consoled us with his optimistic and encouraging words that it wouldn't take long for them to find us. It wasn't our fault; it was the fault of others. And they had to take responsibility for all of us, because they were the guilty ones whom we should certainly count on to relieve us of our responsibility.

You would look all around for resources, and you would see the sky with the sun, the shy October sun. There was plenty of snow that we would melt with that little bit of sun to make water.

The black rocks, sharp and bare, told you of the absence of any plant or animal life, since not even a fly flew in such places. The fuselage, our house, which sheltered us from the wind, and where we spent the night, was our most important resource, because in some way it was our home: the human group that is always, and in all circumstances, the most valuable resource!

In the end, we would complete the inventory another day, as we still didn't know how many of us there were. Because Guido Magri and Daniel Shaw, among many others, had been travelling in the back of the plane, and that part – the tail – had remained up above, though we didn't know where. We were thinking that they might be alive, but it wasn't likely... Maybe they had stayed alive a few hours, but... sleeping up there, scattered all around? Because the tail had catapulted to the other side of the summit, and they had either flown out or had remained inside the tail which had fallen with such violence.

On the mountain, I felt that I had no air, I had difficulty breathing. And night-time fell so suddenly, so abruptly. Not only did it come all at once, it also came quite early in the evening. And then the temperature would plummet.

I speak a lot about the night because it reminded me more of my previous life. I would gaze up at the moon and the stars and reflect that this was what I used to see from my house. The night sky was the link. And you would see something move – I don't know whether I already had something of the artist in me – but you would see something move and it was the clouds that were passing in front of the stars. Sometimes they moved lightly and rapidly, and at other times very slowly. The clouds were playing games with the stars in the stationary window of the plane, through which I would see them pass – first they would let you see them, and then they wouldn't. And the moon… when it was full you could see all around and the night was measured out by the time it took to move from one window to the next. I no longer remember how long it took, but I know that I wanted to touch it. I wanted to touch it because it was there, nearby, and the world was so far away from there. And the moon looked over the whole world. As if it were a household object from my previous life. The moon of my house; the moon that I had seen from the fields with my father; the moon that at that very moment could be looking over my mother or my girlfriend, Soledad; or any of those whom I loved, who were so far away and yet so close in my memory. That's why the nights provided some comfort. They were a respite from the daily misery. They were the hours during which my lost home seemed closer, when the improvised home we had built displayed all the peace and intimacy of its protection.

But then, by day, you would say; "No! This is not my environment!" Daytime was frightening. Night-time seemed more like before. Granted, I was in a broken fuselage, uncomfortable, tightly packed, hungry and thirsty. But at night, it was as if I were lying on my bed at home looking up at those same clouds through my window. And by day, it was like being on another planet. Except occasionally when I came to appreciate the beauty of the mountains. Yes, there were those moments when your soul was at peace. Even beauty can be appreciated ephemerally.

There was nothing left of the past when it wasn't night-time. Up there, you became close to your instincts, as if suddenly making a new friend. Nothing was left of the place inhabited by men!

Then, by chance, we found a transistor radio on which, one morning, we heard the news that as good as said: "Boys, we are calling off the search, we are assuming you are dead, you no longer exist." It's hard to hear about your own death, and it makes you cry out: "No, dammit, I'm alive!"

That was a very hard blow. The reality that they had given us up for dead and were not going to search for us any longer.

But on the other hand, it roused us to stop waiting for others, and to begin to do something ourselves to avoid dying, and to start looking at the possibility of getting out of the mountains on our own. We were left with no other choice! We were upset, and at times furious with the world for confirming something unproven as true.

The first sixteen days

That gave rise to a transformation in our whole attitude. We forgot about the world and our previous lives, and began to develop our new society in the snow!

The stock of food that existed in the plane, which had been distributed equally among the twenty-nine of us, was already exhausted, leaving the rational mind to conclude that we would die of hunger. We would die by not getting the energy that food would provide. Not from the cold, not from thirst, but from starvation.

The only resources we had access to were: snow, rocks, and men, alive as well as dead.

And you think about the dead body of your friend, that there and only there is the protein that will give you the energy to be able to carry on living, and in this way, perhaps, to cross the cordillera in search of that previous life, which is already lost and sometimes seems rather alien. And from it being so much on your mind, there comes a point when you decide to share your secret. And what a shock when the other boy tells you that he's been thinking exactly the same thought for days! You're not sure of your own voice, but you do acknowledge what the other boy is saying. And so, in small groups at first, and then in a general meeting, twenty-year-old boys begin to argue from a legal, moral, religious, theological, and above all from a nutritional, point of view, about the need for all of us to use the dead bodies, empty of their souls, as food.

This idea began to get shared among small groups of friends, because there was nothing left: no chocolates, no jam, no drinks, nothing.

When I first heard someone talk about that possibility, I wasn't at all surprised, because that's what had been passing through my mind. Then we all met in an assembly and the subject was discussed formally.

Points were argued for and against. Any argument against inexorably collided against the wall of death.

We had to defend and honour the life that had been given back to us. The miracle of being alive when logic dictated that we should all be dead.

In that way, some quickly, and others more gradually, took the decision to turn to the bodies for food. I witnessed a pact; the most honourable, dignified, and sincere pact that I have ever seen or been part of, where men pledged to offer themselves to each other in the event of their death, so that the others could live. A pact of deep love between men; love more than feeling. Love realized by human behaviour; and which expresses all human condition, hence the pride I felt and feel in being a man.

As with all decisions, it was discussed and argued for and against. And even more so as this was no ordinary decision, it was very difficult and very tough, and it implied 'life', but when a decision is taken in a group, there is synergy, and already one plus one is not two, it is much more.

We had survived the accident and we had to defend that miracle. We had to do everything we could to retain the possibility of getting out of there and being reunited with our families, our friends, our attachments, and our places. Any sacrifice was worth it.

And so a sacred pact was sealed between men. "If I die, you make use of my body to stay alive," and vice versa. No one knew who would be the next one to die.

This intimate pact was being gradually accepted at different rates and times; some earlier, others later. But everyone ended up accepting it. We feel that it is similar to how, these days, one can prolong a person's life through the donation of a vital organ. We were breaking a taboo.

A taboo is something that one carries deep inside. It was with extreme difficulty that we broke that taboo. We argued religiously, citing the symbol of Jesus at the last supper; also legally, in that there was no law preventing it. Morally, we were not doing anything unscrupulous, or disrespectful, from the moment that we had also offered ourselves to the others. And we argued from the physical and medical points of view that we needed protein to regain energy.

But it is undeniable that the human mind is not prepared to process such a possibility. Mental confusion... pain in the soul... inability to proceed when confronted with the necessity of doing so. Contradictions... but only that pact between men showed me what dignity and integrity are!

All the days of my life I've had to make decisions, but this was surely the most difficult, the hardest, where your mind must force your body to do what you've already decided. But I never thought it was going to be so hard to actually carry out this rational decision. And to force myself to do so.

Because there is a huge space – like the mountains that surrounded us – between making a decision and executing it. Because at first your hand doesn't obey your mind's command, and it must make a superhuman effort to submit to that authority. Then the process is repeated when your mouth won't open to allow yourself to insert the small piece of frozen flesh that your hand finally took. And later still when your throat refuses to swallow it.

And this effort of mind over body took me a few days. But when that process reached its conclusion, I felt that I was saved, through that communion with the body and blood of my friends. How far we had come!

The process of arguing to live was undertaken with the noble, ethical and worthy intent of saving the body, but it had another face, the humiliated soul, because no other animal eats its own species. At times, the act seemed aberrant, and death seemed the way to go rather than anthropophagy. So, it was always difficult for me to swallow; I would keep on retching, and the same thing would happen to Numa and to others.

But what a capacity man has to adapt, as I vividly remember people eating, though not the small frozen pieces, but the other parts, which I have chosen not to write about so as not to cause any distress. That image is from much later than the initial anthropophagy. What primitivism! It seemed as if our free will was no longer recognizable, or had disappeared. And instinct had replaced it!

'Cannibalism' is a word that describes the Caribs of the Lesser Antilles; indigenous people who supposedly had the habit of feeding on human flesh after killing the victim (although this claim is disputed by historians and by descendants of the islanders).

'Necrophagy' comes from the Greek 'nekros' (dead body) and refers to the eating of human bodies that are already dead. It does not necessarily refer to a habitual practice, and, as happened to us, we participated in necrophagy only because there was no other option. And that's how it should be understood, that this word does not connote habit, and even less so, killing in order to eat.

In the Andes, I participated in necrophagy as the only option to stay alive. I was nourished by the bodies of my friends who had already died, and that was my only chance of staying alive and fulfilling the dream of returning to the affections of my family. But not before first offering the others my own body in the case of my own death.

If someone routinely confuses these terms and calls everyone who has eaten human flesh a cannibal, he is wrong. On some occasions, we have been wrongly branded as such, and we want to point out the differences.

When we returned to Uruguay on 28ᵗʰ December 1972, at a worldwide press conference we accepted and admitted to this fact, with sorrow, but without guilt.

It cost me dear to make the decision but it was much more difficult to actually go through with it. I could not have done so, but every day my friends forced me to eat. I lost forty-five kilograms, that is to say half of my weight. And when they rescued me I had only a couple of days of life left in me due to starvation. Everyone was more or less in agreement about that.

The most terrible thing for me to overcome was the fact that they were my dead friends. What allowed me to do it, among other things, was the intimate pact between us. That commitment full of love, of one for another. No one knew who would be the next to die.

The attitude which was then determination, was born out of a feeling of enormous respect and great love among all of us. "If I die, I would like you to take my body to continue living."

"No man can have greater love than to lay down his life for his friends."

(Saint John)

Even though that is not something that we chose to do. We only fulfilled the duty that we faced in life... to carry on living!

They also didn't choose it, just as we didn't choose it. No one sacrificed themselves, dying to give life to another. That didn't happen. God or destiny decided it, and that choice or criterion cannot be known or understood. It is a mystery. I have spent the last forty-eight years of my life asking it myself and I still haven't reached any conclusion. And I never will.

What does move me is the love with which the sacred pact was made, and I think that it was my inner conflict that was the most difficult thing to overcome. And I think that this unbroken pact of communion is the common denominator among the survivors forever! It is what unites us despite our differences.

The first sixteen days

And so I took care of the others, I helped to cut meat with my friends. With the Strauch cousins, because I was a friend of theirs. And a friend of the younger boys. Unlike Pedro, I didn't have any problems integrating into the group; on the contrary, it was the easiest thing of all to become part of it. And this was despite my being one of the older ones and not having gone to Stella Maris College.

I functioned as a unifier, and I would calm the hysteria and depression. But first I would calm myself. 'This is the situation,' I would say to myself, 'and the problems that arise need to be solved.'

Initially, when they were talking at night about the food, I was considering death as an alternative. I didn't want to eat, until I was persuaded by the boys' arguments.

First, I would take care of myself, and later I would be available for the others. I was going through a process of despair and of anguish, which was a constant feature for all of us. And you would turn to some, or to others, always talking to them. And at night you could see the glow of the cigarettes. It was more silent after saying the Rosary. You talked to God, and when you make a prayer, when you pray, God talks to you. I'm not sure which did me the more good – taking care of myself first, or taking care of the others.

It was what we were doing and what we did on each and every one of those interminable days we lived on the mountain. We would eat the ration that they gave us, and eat constantly what was freely available like a cow grazing all day. When the time came to distribute the meat, carefully cut, initially, into small rationed portions, it was not to satisfy our hunger, which we had already painfully experienced, but to ingest some of the energy that would prolong life.

You would conserve a little bit of energy, or at least try to do so, by keeping quiet. Just getting up to urinate was such an effort that it left me breathless. I suppose that those who went out walking to explore the surroundings ate much more than me, since the effort needed to move at those heights was superhuman. Both my legs felt very heavy, breathing was an effort in itself, and it seemed as if my chest would explode with the slightest additional work.

We talked of family life. I well remember my talks with the team captain Marcelo about returning home and going out to eat with our mothers. We also talked about our situation, guessing where we could be, and what were the different options for getting out of there. And we discussed all kinds of practical solutions for our coexistence on the mountain.

Communion

This is the same hand that reached out to us from the beginning. It holds a human body and a chalice... body and blood which defend and honour life and beyond. The communion that allowed us to live.

There are mountains in the background and they are seen as through a window, or a host. It is a sacramental image and was painted for an exhibition of religious themes. I have always felt that it represents much more than meets the eye!

I had a discussion with Nando about God and he said to me, "How can I believe in God when my mother and my sister died there?" And I say, "But you saved yourself, Nando, and I was saved – everyone should have died." And he answered, "But you returned to your house and everyone was there; I returned to mine and had nobody." "No, no, I had already lost my father six years previously. You have your dad and it was for him that you did all that you did."

So, thanks be to God, sixteen of us returned – that is the miracle. Because we should all be dead. And later, people understood or misunderstood what happened there. But someone who understood was Fito. Fito Strauch today when he speaks of these things, talks about them as I do. We agree closely in our view of what happened!

The first sixteen days

At night, conflicts were settled with punches or kicks, with promises to continue the following morning. Later, they were forgotten about because they were not serious conflicts but trifles relating to positional comfort, since we spent the nights squashed up very tightly against each other.

I would think about my house and my mother, about Soledad, my sisters and brother, and my old friends. So dear to me! What would they be eating if they were having breakfast, or what would they be doing? And I would compare it to what I was experiencing and I wouldn't have wanted to tell them even if it had been possible.

Who would take care of my family?

It had been a while since my youth had given way to responsibility, denying me the casual choices that would have been typical for an eighteen-year-old. Until I got on to that damn plane! And to then experience the worst situations imaginable, that I would not wish on my worst enemy, if I had one.

And in that new situation in which we found ourselves on the mountain, the result of human error, the easiest thing of all was to integrate into that human group that was still alive. I had friends of my age who were studying agronomy with me, such as Fito Strauch and Daniel Fernandez. In the same way, Eduardo Strauch and Marcelo Pérez were friends who studied architecture together. Pancho Delgado and Numa Turcatti were companions of Gastón – all law students. And I fitted in very quickly, and from the very first moment, with the younger ones, because, even though they were just nineteen, they were beginning to show what a man must do when the circumstances demand it.

I owe all of them my life because they took care of me and even pampered me during those seventy-two days on the mountain. They worried about me, in a situation where every individual was struggling to survive another day. It is to them that I owe everything I have, because they helped me get to 22nd December still alive, giving me another chance to start living life to the full again. Which I most certainly have done!

Breaking a taboo

I did this drawing in June 2002. It is completely figurative so is easily understood.

It is a typical scene, occurring daily, in which a few boys are complaining about what needs to be done; others are very calmly doing it; I imagine that the boy carrying the food is the team captain.

Each person took their daily ration, which came around already prepared in small mounds. The tray was prepared on the other side of the aircraft.

It represents much more than what is shown. It is the execution of a decision already taken, the only way to defend and honour life, thus breaking a taboo which was rooted deep within each of us.

For me, it was the most intimate communion, painful, and cruel, but what my mind forced me to do to survive. And when I did it for the first time - which was extremely difficult – I was saved; it had the taste of hope.

chapter III Life and memory

We had become well-known figures, loved by the public; something that continued to surprise us. People would greet us on the street, and they wouldn't let us pay for anything in the shops.

My physical recovery was so rapid that, within those few days in Santiago, I managed to gain ten kilos.

As soon as we landed at Carrasco airport in Montevideo, we were taken by the Christian Brothers to Stella Maris College, where they informed us that there would be a press conference with journalists from all over the world! Thanks to the intervention of our dear Uruguayan journalist Cristina Moran, they agreed that each of us would tell the story of our odyssey in the cordillera, but no-one would ask questions. We would then be free to return to our homes, which was what we wanted most.

Many people were waiting in my house and I don't remember at what time I finally retired to my much-missed bed. My mother took over my brother's bed, which was next to mine, and she spent the night there in vigil, listening to me breathe.

As I was accustomed to sleeping for only short periods, it didn't take me long to wake up and I was filled with a sudden need to draw those things that I had no wish to talk about. It was all so intimate and so recent! But the great happiness of being alive filled my soul. I was off that mountain, and in my home, with my family and my friends; reasons that up there had given meaning to life, making the pain, the anguish, and the despair a little more bearable, even a bit more dignified, which had prevented the humiliation taking over.

Why, on that night of 28th December, did I draw what I experienced, rather than talk about it with my mother and friends?

I think it was because it was easier for me. I held the images very close in time, and very clear; and my hand was drawing almost without thinking. It was just me and the drawings, there was no other participant in the conversation, and the emotion flowed directly between me and the paper.

Conserving Energy

I did this drawing on the night of 28th December 1972. The day on which we returned to Uruguay having spent five days in Santiago, Chile, where it hadn't seemed real that we were back to civilization, enjoying comfort and good food, and in the company of our families with whom we shared Christmas Eve and Christmas Day.

At that moment in time, I wasn't able to share the experience. I knew that I might break down, overcome by those sad memories, which for me were still harrowing, open wounds. It was very difficult to talk about it without being moved to tears. It was all very intimate, and mine alone.

It has always been a bit difficult for me to speak from the soul, but I also could not convey anything that wasn't from the soul. Memories, so close and so fresh, would surface, and everything would give me a lot of pain once again.

Capturing an image on paper was always simpler, without anyone else involved; without showing emotions or feelings. In short, without exposing what I felt to the judgment of the others, without emotional effort, and without having to choose adequate words to describe it. Also, it exhausted me to talk about what I had experienced. In fact, I just wanted to forget...

Life and memory

People in Montevideo seemed to speak very loudly and move very fast. It was so noisy that it scared me sometimes. I was also getting overwhelmed by a lot of care and attention, to the point where I decided to go to the farm. That was where I found my true environment and where I later settled down and raised my family.

After eight months, I married my girlfriend Soledad – I was so excited to be starting my own family! A new family that, so many times on the mountain, I thought I would never have...

At that time, I also graduated as an agronomist, and I turned my attention to milk production, and to feeling the pleasure of being alive; to enjoying life, to being able to just turn on a tap to drink water, to eating a variety of foods, to sleeping in a bed with a pillow, and to seeing a fire in the hearth. And all this together with my beloved lifelong companion, who after a year of marriage gave me the most emotional and intense moment that I've ever experienced in my life when she gave birth to our first son, José Luis, on 7th June 1974.

And to think that I imagined there could be no more intense moment than when those two helicopters came flying over to rescue us on 22nd December 1972.

To experience what, so many times on the mountain, I thought I would never experience! To have started a family! That was the main need of those seventy-two days: family, friends, and the places that I loved.

This common objective was all just a dream, and everything was done and endured in pursuit of it. To escape from there to be with my family, and to form my own family, was what I wanted most.

Afterwards, life proceeded normally, just as with any person who had not lived through such an extreme experience. Soledad and I have three wonderful children: José Luis, Maria Soledad, and Maria Eugenia.

They are my greatest treasure and the best gift I have received in life, together with life itself.

After graduating in agronomy in 1973, I worked for thirty-five years on one of my family's dairy establishments. I also did some independent work, though always linked to milk production and, to a lesser degree, agriculture.

Later, I formed the National Association of Milk Producers, and in 1987 I was elected a director of Conaprole, the dairy cooperative in my country, remaining on their board until 1997.

Family (2006)

These days I have the farm leased out, and with the extra time I have at my disposal, I decided to dabble in the world of art by way of oil painting. That was also a dream that I hadn't yet realized.

So I have dedicated myself to painting for more than fifteen years now, and this continues to give me a lot of satisfaction. In these paintings, I describe memories of the mountain and, also, any other rural and urban experiences that come to mind.

None of us has suffered psychological consequences of what we experienced, since we did the therapy up there, all together, each supporting the others. Seventy-two days was a lot of time for us to adapt to that environment, and to adapt to what we had to go through. And that is the wonder of human beings, our ability to adapt...

There were a few physical consequences. Some were left a bit lame by broken legs that had fused together on the mountain; others had burnt retinas from exposure to the reflection of the sun off the snow and have had to have retinal transplants to avoid losing their sight.

But these were trifles compared to the circumstances through which they had lived, and they were able to cope with them easily.

I don't know if anyone else has gone through a similar experience to ours. That is not to say that no-one has experienced anything worse. There are wars and horrors in the world which pit men against men. We fought against nature, but it was an incredibly tough and prolonged struggle.

I think that seventy-two days out of my seventy-two years are nothing, but how intense they were! There was nothing in my life as deep and intense as that, except, most importantly, the day that my first child was born!

They were seventy-two tragic days, but there were also more transcendent moments, which I have never experienced or felt again, and which I am neither able to nor want to forget. Moments that made me feel proud to be a human being, and to share with others the miracle of life.

My wife constantly takes care of me as if I were a child, my three beloved children also take care of me and worry about me, and I have eight grandchildren. And just seeing them gives me as much joy as one can possibly have at this age.

I don't study as I used to, but instead of accompanying my father I am accompanied by my children, my grandchildren, my sweet partner in life Soledad, and by my lifelong friends. They are old like me, but we are able to remember it all.

I have received so much that I think that it's not fair, because I have always been unable to give back as much as I have received.

Giving

There are many forms of giving and of giving oneself. On the mountain, there was nothing to give because we had nothing. But one could give in many different ways.

It wasn't like down here in the everyday world, where you can give a few pesos to anyone who asks, or give food to the hungry, or give your time to those who need help, with a smile and a willingness to listen and talk. It is also possible to give thanks, to recognize what you have received from someone else.

Gratitude is a recompense, a recognition, and is also a form of giving that engenders a circle of encounters and of unity. And certainly, all of this happens! But sometimes man focuses on the having rather than the giving.

Memories of the Andes

And in those seventy-two days in the Andes, we were so poor that there was nothing to give – I mean nothing material – because we didn't possess anything! But we were getting rich spiritually. And increasingly rich! And that we could certainly share!

I saw how people were willing to give from the very first day. Nobody rushed out in an 'every man for himself' attitude. Everyone attended to the wounded who were crying out for help, offering the only thing we had: comfort through our words, and a caress to let them know that they weren't alone.

The making of water is an example of selfless giving. I remember Arturo Nogueira inside the fuselage, melting snow drop-by-drop on a sunny October day, and after hours and hours, almost filling a bottle with a liquid made pink from the dregs of the wine.

He gave it to the first boy, who took a sip, and the bottle was successively passed along from mouth to mouth. That took place when there were still twenty-seven of us who had survived the accident. And by the time the bottle had returned to Arturo, it was already empty, and he hadn't drunk any of it! And he knew that if the sun didn't reappear the next day, he wouldn't be able to make more water.

He had transformed the dripping snow into something as valuable as water, and had given it to his companions so that they could minimally quench their thirst, and then he had waited until it had done the full round before bringing it to his own lips, at which point there was no longer a drop left.

That is true giving of oneself, with love, with a strong sense of caring, and it implies great generosity and sacrifice!

Necessity sparks creativity, and to share what has been created is also to give. The example we had was Fito, our friend who, up there in the cordillera, with great intelligence and imagination, managed to invent the things we needed in those limited circumstances, and he offered them to everyone to ease their pains and sorrows. He devised a way to make water, he fabricated lenses to provide protection from the sun, and various other things. That was giving to others so that they didn't suffer like him.

Yes – giving of himself. Because he cherished you, he loved you so much; as much as, or more than, himself.

For that reason, I refer to those who shared the Andes experience with me as my fellow companions. During the seventy-two days on the mountain, they were my intimate equals, much more than friends.

A fellow companion does not judge you, does not point the finger at you; he only loves you as himself, or even more so. He gives to you, he helps you, he supports you, without requiring anything in return. He thinks of you and teaches you to imitate him.

Digging up bodies after the avalanche, which had completely covered the fuselage and killed several of us, was giving oneself for others. Doing it with lacerated hands painful from the ice, bursting your lungs with the effort. Feeling the anguish and the depression for the other's life, which we knew was worth just as much as our own.

The expeditionaries, Nando, Tintín and Roberto, showed us what giving oneself means at a bigger scale. Crossing the cordillera on foot! The effort was an extreme feat in that they didn't hesitate to risk their own lives to save all of us.

We had companions who clearly died from giving and giving of themselves. That was the case with Numa Turcatti, who died on 11th December 1972, because in giving himself he expended so much more energy than the little he was able to receive in return. His energy balance was completely negative. He was an exceptional man.

It is because of these examples, and many more, that I say that the way of man begins and ends with giving and giving oneself without demanding anything in return.

Fundamentally, giving to others is also a form of giving to ourselves; not in order to get something back, but for the satisfaction and unity that it brings. We are a mirror that reflects our own image. And that unity manifests itself in the absence of loneliness, which, without doubt, is not what man is made for: to live in solitude.

Reciprocity comes automatically, because sooner or later you will get your reward, receiving something from the other. But there is recompense in just being on the road that leads to peace and to the truth, and on that road you give yourself to others and you will also receive from others, because you are not alone. And that surely gives meaning to life!

Restraint

During the first sixteen days after the accident, when I was healthy, I wanted to take care of the others, despite not having the physical capacity to support my efforts. Yes, there were attacks of hysteria. Someone would say to one of the others: "Do something," and that person would set out to do it in a mad frenzy, throwing things everywhere. At that point I would go to him and hug him and say, "Stop! Be quiet! Sit down and rest! Do things calmly!"

Memories of the Andes

One night, I dreamt that I was in my great-uncle's house in Buenos Aires, on Corrientes Street, and I was lying between the wall and the floor, just as we did in the plane. A delirious dream. And I was there with a friend, and suddenly I woke up and I was actually beating Alvarito Mangino's broken leg. One punch after another, and he was howling. It wasn't a hysterical attack, it was delirium; a very rare dream. Probably due to lack of water.

There were moments of great anguish, which, these days, we would call panic attacks. Crises of anxiety that would happen one after another up there. Anguish was a common denominator that existed among us. Another common denominator was the need to resolve conflicts.

I remember someone who was crying; I don't recall who. It was night-time ... you sense that someone is sobbing but you don't see his face. You don't move closer to him because you cannot see, and you would end up stepping on everyone if you tried to reach him. But you tell him, "Hey, whoever's sniffling, are you thinking about your home? About everything that you miss? Look, we are here now, trying to get through this endless night, this is the reality."

The goal was to get him to accept the reality; a reality that was incredibly challenging but the only one we had. And I kept saying, "Leave all that in the past. Don't waste time regretting what happened. We will figure out how to deal with what has happened to us."

That was the point. That was the argument. How to deal with what had happened to you, however difficult it was. So we lived with the constant conflict between reasoning, helping, and receiving.

There were others of a different temperament, a different character, who would sometimes get angry and shout.

And for anyone who was faltering, you would make them see that what they were crying for was far away and belonged to the past. It had already taken place.

This was not a place where humans dwelt. We were very far away from anywhere inhabitable. I told them, "We are here in a place where no one lives, and yet we are alive. We must thank God every day for that! The miracle of being alive when we should all be dead!"

In Uruguay, they had given us up for dead, because that's what logic dictated. Although afterwards I heard that my mother had never agreed to consider me dead.

And when the boys listened to this kind of reasoning, they reconsidered. They were all intelligent and reasonable people. Talented people, who put all their talent and their intelligence to the service of others. But, understandably, they would suddenly lose themselves – in their memories, in the brutal distress in which they were permanently living, and in resolving conflicts.

Fito helped me like a mother, constantly. He brought me water and food. He took care that I didn't exchange it for cigarettes. He was always the companion who looked after me and who pampered me the most. But it is terrible when one becomes weak and dependent; a condition that, for me, was aggravated by developing gangrene in one leg.

I contained my depression and constant conflicts because we were never at peace up there – one couldn't ever be at peace. Because when dawn came, when you saw the daybreak through those oval windows, you would thank God for allowing you to get through the night! But then, would you be able to make it through the day? The same conflict returning... and what could you do? Conserve energy? You couldn't do much. The days were long and the hours dragged on. And you had to eat the bodies of your dead friends.

Others did not experience the conflict so much. And they were strong because they ate a lot, otherwise they wouldn't have been able to cross the cordillera as did those two towers of strength, Nando and Roberto.

But for me, it was horrible. I always had a total revulsion for what I was doing. I ate less and less, and, after I was left disabled, I ate less still because I wasn't expending any energy. I had hardly anything to replenish.

I also took care not to drive everyone crazy, because madness is contagious; and a lot of humour was needed.

There is a photo, and a follow-up one, where I said to Daniel: "Hey, lift up your head and smile for the camera as someone in your household might see it one day. So that they see you smiling, and not all downcast." And he did it, and that picture is precious. I'm hugging Pancho, who is also smiling, and it looks like I am raising Daniel's head.

Pancho also told some very funny stories. At which point you would laugh, relax, and forget where you were for a while.

It was the same when we said the Rosary; something that Carlitos required of us. And we also made up prayers. And because we didn't remember the Salve Regina

Memories of the Andes

(Hail Holy Queen) too well, we pieced it together bit by bit from our collective memories, and nowadays I pray it every day. It is our official prayer, and it came together with the help of everyone, and it mentions the Valley of Tears, which we later learned was the name of our location on the mountain.

My role as caregiver must have been influenced by my close experience of death, my father having died six years earlier. So I think that my father helped me greatly in an intangible way.

And I suppose also that my father will have taught me about giving and giving oneself, which I must have absorbed and internalized without even realizing it. I knew how to care... and he had taught me!

I also felt his presence in the avalanche. I think that he helped me with my mental strength. You can explain mental strength as the thing that gives mental order to chaos, like painting a picture from a chaotic photograph – you can simplify it. Like when you set about analysing and solving a problem – you attack the easiest part first, but beyond that, nothing is simple.

I remembered when my father, walking around the dairy farm, had shown me all that there was, the multitude of Holstein cows and the many facilities that had been built up over time, with dedication and effort. "You see, Cochemba, here there was nothing," he would tell me, and that taught me how much the will and imagination of human beings can achieve.

There are many people who have imagination but not everyone achieves what has been imagined. And one must pity the people who don't even have a creative imagination; or who cannot carry things through. Because it really does require a lot of effort and sacrifice. And with the mind you give place and meaning to that sacrifice.

That is strength. When your mind controls your body, because I imagine that Nando and Roberto must have strained their knees a few times when they were walking and climbing without proper equipment, not knowing whether they would reach an inhabited place.

"Pull yourself together and suffer a bit more," said Nando's father when he was rowing. "I suffered a while longer, you make some sacrifices. Give to others, for yourself and for them." Because a person in authority must make sacrifices.

I use the word 'authority' rather than 'leadership'. People with authority sacrifice many things – some for loss and some for gain – but the great sacrifice entailed by authority is implicit, because it is done for others.

"Smile!"

Smiles All Round

The humour, and the jokes that we made! Suddenly one of us would say, "Hey stop, Liliana is here," and as the only woman in the group, and wife of Javier Methol who was also there, she would reply, "No, boys, please carry on." She would be killing herself laughing. "Please don't stop." She meant a lot to us, and it was a great loss when she died in the avalanche.

Memories of the Andes

For a start, their vocation to serve demands many sacrifices. To leave your family, to attend to others, and to forgo the chance to sit down and have a quiet drink.

Roberto Canessa fulfilled that role during the sixty-two days prior to the hike. Nando Parrado also assumed the same role during that time. And among those who remained in the fuselage waiting, with great uncertainty, to see if Parrado and Canessa would achieve their goal of finding help, the role of authority was taken on by the Strauch cousins, including Fito.

They tell me that I had authority, but I don't know. Because I didn't tell anything to Piers Paul Read, the author of the book *Alive*. Pablo Gelsi, the interpreter, said to me, "You told him nothing!" I told him three bits of nonsense, nothing more. What comes out in the book about me is from what others said.

There were previous moments of my life which helped me on the mountain. The image of my father dying, with my grandfather crying over him, was something indelible for me. Lifting up my head in the plane after the crash, and seeing the disaster, surrounded by the dead and the cries that were slowly growing louder as if someone were turning up the volume... Because at first there had been an absolute silence and when I raised my head... moans, cries and screams. That also made a deep impression.

In both cases I raised my head, and I was fully conscious of what was happening. "My father is dying." And then, after the desperate attempts of my grandfather to give him artificial respiration, I was aware that my father had just died. And then again, when I saw my mother crying bitterly I thought that I would try to help her bear the pain, by looking after her and the family. And likewise, on the mountain, I told myself, "I'm going to take care of them, my new family."

The death of my father when I was eighteen was my first and largest blow. It was different to that of the mountain, because it seems to me as though I hold something of my father deep within me, much more so than the tragedy that I experienced in the Andes. I am realizing that now.

The other day, at dawn, when I wrote about my father, I did it with pleasure! It was gratifying, as if we were meeting up again. That happens often, when I visit the cemetery to chat. By contrast, writing about the mountain was horrible. It was extremely distressing.

chapter IV The last fifty-six days

The avalanche

I said previously that the days after the accident could not have been worse. But, on 29th October, after having been abandoned on the mountain, I discovered that, however bad your situation is, it can always get worse.

I don't think I have the words to describe the horror. On that date, sixteen days after disaster, we suffered the worst thing that happened to us in the cordillera. Or perhaps it wasn't the worst, but it was certainly one of the hardest blows, following on from so many others that had brought us to a state of extreme weakness, completely diminishing our strength and leaving us emotionally at rock bottom. Because, from the moment that we knew we had been abandoned, the fight had become extremely ruthless.

It was late evening and we were already all inside the fuselage with our 'house' in reasonable order. That was when our team captain, Marcelo, asked to swap places with me. The places rotated daily and on that night it was my turn to have one of the better ones. He, on the other hand, had quite a bad one, up against the communication equipment at the front right of the fuselage, where the icy wind would enter.

Of course, I had no great desire to change but the request came from our captain whom I loved very much and whom I had admired from the start for his behaviour, and for all the good that he had imparted to me in our one-to-one conversations. So I agreed and changed places with him and ended up lying next to Bobby François and facing Fito.

Suddenly, there was a sound like a team of 300 horses galloping towards us from a distance. I looked towards the opening in the fuselage, which was walled up with all sorts of things and suddenly everything flew inwards like an explosion and landed on top of us, followed by tons of snow that trapped our bodies.

Memories of the Andes

The roar of an approaching avalanche doesn't give you time to react; you see that flash of white for a second and immediately you find yourself buried under metres of snow.

You struggle one more time, you try to get out and free yourself from that huge weight, but it's impossible. It squeezes you with an almighty force, it robs you of oxygen, and from then on you feel that you can hardly breathe... and to breathe is to live!

Then the snow immediately became compacted and imprisoned us, leaving us unable to move.

Fito's foot on my face was forming a small capsule of air, but I was completely immobilized. A second compaction of the snow compressed me so much that it made me urinate.

In a situation like that, you become aware of the force with which you have to contend. But you understand clearly that everything will end that way: in a few minutes we would be buried alive. The cold also starts to impair your mind. Immobilized and with almost no oxygen, your body surrenders; you understand that there is nothing more you can do. And, paradoxically, not being able to fight any longer gives you a certain peace. No more pain, no more struggle, only controlling the small amount of oxygen remaining; immobile, constrained as if in a straightjacket, knowing that you are dying, that death is coming, that there is nothing more you can do.

How many minutes will it take? Your own anxiety degrades your ability to control the little oxygen that remains; and the awareness that death is coming in a few moments paralyzes you even more.

Everything was ending, and then... I think of my father, who is waiting for me, and Gastón. And that anguish and desperation is transformed, in a split second, into the most genuine peace that I have ever felt in my life. I am reuniting with my father, whom I missed so much. There, dying happy and at peace, I am about to embrace my dear dad.

Suddenly, Fito's foot moves away from my face, leaving a tunnel that allows the air to flow back into my lungs, and just like a newborn with a scream or a cry, I come back to life. My lungs slowly fill with oxygen... and I am born again!

I had a flash of doubt as to whether to go with my father to that paradise of peace and happiness, or to return to this life of constant suffering, albeit one that I knew and believed to be worth living.

The last fifty-six days

What had happened? Fito, who had his foot on my face, on being rescued by Roy, had left an air channel; an open pathway to life. And that new life is desperate to fight once more, it is almost atavistic, the struggle for survival compels one to act, and I managed to get out of that grave.

I emerged from that cold tomb and returned to the chaos. The earlier fear and paralysis turned into the desperation of helping the rest of my companions to live. And with an unimaginable effort, I returned to fight alongside the others in this race against time.

We dug like animals to allow the others to live. We dug with the only tools we had – our hands, hurt and cut by the ice but already numb to the pain, our lungs at the point of exploding from the incredible effort.

We tried to uncover just their faces so that they could breathe. We passed in an instant from the joy of having found someone to the immense sadness of finding it was too late to revive them.

Cries, pleas for help to dig towards those who were buried and dying, and who were just as important to me as myself.

The space inside the fuselage had been reduced to a minimum. Everything was full of compacted snow. Digging at full speed, doglike, in hardened snow, hurts your fingers, and the effort sets your heart racing at full speed. But you cannot stop because your friend is dying there below.

I uncovered Bobby's face, still alive, followed immediately by another, already dead! Marcelo, not long dead, in the place where I should have been. Javier cried out for Liliana, who was also dead. Later, we extricated Pancho, Numa and another – I don't remember who – and they were alive. It was a frantic race against time and death, where the logic of reason cannot explain why some lived and others did not. It is a mystery to this day.

We lost eight friends in the avalanche, including Liliana, the only woman in the group.

The mountain was giving birth to them

We were there inside the fuselage for three days, pressed up against the roof in a bubble of air surrounded by snow and ice. It was worse than anything; horrific, terrible, just suffering and more suffering. Without oxygen, the living and the dead squeezed up against one another without the possibility of even stretching a leg.

Everything dark, not knowing whether it was day or night. The only good thing was that that it wasn't so cold, since in an igloo protected from the wind, the temperature goes to 0° Celsius; considerably warmer than a night on the snow outside.

The fuselage had been completely covered by snow, and only after piercing the roof with a tube that appeared out of nowhere (I believe that God is behind that coincidence) were we able to restore our air supply, which was almost exhausted, as was made evident by the sputtering flame of a lighter.

Our clothes were soaked through and our despair grew because we thought that now no one would ever find us.

The avalanche

This is an abstract painting because I only saw the avalanche for a split second. Afterwards, everything was darkness and silence.

Hands are upraised as if wanting to stem that avalanche. Then the worst began, and afterwards everything changed!

The last fifty-six days

Some of us had survived for a second time, but perhaps we would still all die, buried alive inside that wreck of a fuselage, covered by snow.

We also had to feed ourselves from the bodies of our friends who had just died, since the other bodies had all disappeared under tons of snow.

The immobility of those days gave me gangrene in my right leg, and with that, everything changed for me. I had confronted death one more time, but it was now different for me. In the avalanche, I had that experience of feeling myself dying, and that was when I saw my father. Then, after having lived through something like that, a change takes place, because death stops being the worst thing that can happen to you. And from then on, I lost all fear and I found freedom in that cold white prison; a freedom that liberates you... and gives rise to truth, goodness, and peace!

On the third day, we started to dig a tunnel towards the cockpit. We had to go through the door in the middle, and then turn to the left towards the window to the side of one of the dead pilots.

As we dug, we threw the snow back over ourselves, as there wasn't any other free space. After hours of hard work digging that tunnel, which turned out to be quite a feat of engineering, we came to the window and then began another huge task, which was to kick it open in order to get out, which took quite a while.

When we finally got it open, we found that the snow covering it was loose, so without too much effort we started our ascent.

And from that damp, confined black hole where we had found ourselves condemned and reduced to the worst dregs of humanity, I saw a ray of light entering, and one after another we began to crawl through the tunnel, following the bright new light that was showing us the way. No one could imagine the effect that it had on me to get out and see that new spectacle.

The intense blue sky and a sun that embraced us warmly.

The snow, white and clean, as if it were starched.

The contrast of lights and intense colours that dazzled me after three days of darkness.

The fuselage, and the debris and dirt surrounding it, were no longer there. Everything was white, clean, and immaculate, as if starting afresh. We were in the same place, but one that had been equipped for other people who had been reborn.

Memories of the Andes

Sitting down, and ecstatic about everything new that I saw, I watched my friends emerge from the tunnel one after another, their ragged clothes contrasting against that pristine landscape.

It was as if the mountain were giving birth to them again, through the snow.

But I remember, with great emotion, the sense that someone else was there with us: for the first time, I felt that God was there, and was expressed through the men sitting there. It was Jesus of Nazareth, who lived for thirty-three years, who died on a cross, and who left the world a message more captivating that any man has ever left: "Love one another, as I have loved you." It was and still is the biggest revolution that this world has experienced!

With his divine message, some of the so-called 'sins' of man on earth were dislodged, such as greed, avarice, vanity and deceit, which are virtues to some. And forgiveness, giving and giving of oneself, and truth and mercy emerged through the deeds of men. And love, which discovers the empty soul and fills it with peace and happiness. All fear is put aside and freedom surfaces, which takes you to the truth, and if you travel along that path, you find, at the end of it, the reward of peace. Peace that guided me to the greatest undertaking that I have projected onto my life: to do my best to return to what I desired most – my family and friends... Because when you are alone with your soul, with your life hanging in the balance, and with nothing material to debase it, your family emerges as the most necessary thing, and you want to return to it, because nothing else matters.

And that new birth marked the point at which we started to make smarter decisions, and we began to see the emergence of leaders who, by their readiness to serve, and by working harder and better, guided the rest of us.

Nando, Roberto and Tintín were the chosen expeditionaries, just like the earliest warriors. The Strauch cousins guarded that most precious commodity, our food, like the most primitive of resources. And the rest of us did what was necessary for the others to carry out their tasks, where everyone gave the best of themselves according to their character and their way of doing things.

And so, after a barrage of ideas, it was decided in which direction we would exit, whether it would be to the east or to the west, and who would go, and when.

Night-time

This is another figurative drawing in which you can see how we spent every night, and any day on which there was a storm – semi-reclined, packed tight, and without any great possibility of movement.

Seeing it causes me to relive it, and I swear it was terrible. We gave each other warmth, certainly, but we were sitting ducks in the face of another avalanche. Sometimes we would hear some snow breaking off, and we would jump up like springs.

I make good use of this drawing to show Carlitos tending to my injured leg.

That's how it was, and now forty-eight years have gone by!! I remember that when there was a storm, a lot of wind and snow entered, and the next morning we would wake up covered with a thin layer of white.

To this day, I cannot fathom how we could have endured this for seventy-two days.

It is a very disagreeable memory and vision. Even today, I remember the smell with anguish!

The Resurrection

And we started to establish the logistics to support the tactics and strategies that were taking shape. It was not like a company whose success is measured by its revenue or profits or some other objective. The only goal was to live in order to get out of there and so to be able to realize the dream and desire that which was common to all: the family.

Today, it is very difficult to put into words those sensations and feelings of a divine presence.

Forty-eight years after the fact, it is difficult for one's mind to recreate moments from the past, but I do know and am fully aware of what happened and what I experienced.

And that communion with its common objective was what transformed that human group into a formidable team with all the necessary organization, which everyone respected even though it wasn't written down.

Change of role

But our feet were in contact with the ice throughout that time, which couldn't fail to have consequences.

One day, I woke up with a pain in my leg, and when I rolled up my trousers I saw that it had become swollen. I took off my shoes and socks and saw that the swelling had spread to my toes, which were black. The veins of my right leg had frozen and, as a result, I had developed gangrene, which is caused by anaerobic bacteria.

I was in my fifth year of studying agronomy and had seen gangrenous cow udders, which become black and drooping. Because the bacteria thrive when there is no oxygen, the vet would inject hydrogen peroxide to get rid of the gangrene. That much I knew, as I had learned it on the dairy farm.

Then the swelling began to climb up my leg and at some points it burst. One spot opened up, and then another. And what looked like little islands appeared, even on my toes.

One day, Roberto Canessa passes by and tells me that I have gangrene, and that it is going to spread upwards, and that I'm going to die. "We'll have to cut off your leg," he says. And I thought: 'Wait a minute! He's in his first year of medicine and I'm in my fifth year of agronomy. He is not going to cut off my leg!'

So I said, "Give me a razorblade," and added, "Ah, that's what I was missing. Now, how is it that I'll die of gangrene?" And the next day, Numa developed the same problem. Was it going to happen to all of us? Five days later, after my whole thigh began to swell up, I took the razorblade and opened up a gash in the shape of a cross. It didn't hurt; rather, it was a relief, as jets of bloody pus spurted out. And then I massaged myself. From top to bottom, from thigh to calf. I squeezed down from my thigh and everything emerged below.

I cut myself in order for the pus to exit and for the oxygen to enter. I knew that much. I made a cross so that it would open up more, because if you make a cut, it can close up, but with a cross, there are four ends that need to come together. Then I squeezed and it came out. There was even a day when Javier Methol was eating and I spilt some pus over his food; someone else saw it and kept quiet about it, and Javier ate it all, as if it were a bit of ketchup. Years later, I spoke to Javier about this, and he replied, "Ah, so that's why it was so delicious that day!"

And I couldn't walk anymore after that because it was too painful. I would drag myself out and hobble around in the vicinity of the plane, in pain and oozing pus.

When I returned to Montevideo, my grandfather told me, "These are called torpid ulcers and they'll take a long time to heal."

It took fifteen years. Soledad would help me on with my socks and would bandage me up because I would ooze pus and soil everything.

And so I became reliant on the others and I told myself, 'Sonofabitch, now I can't walk anymore.' And not walking meant I was not expending energy. So I neither had an appetite, nor did I enjoy eating. It was then that Fito made me eat. He brought me water, he attended to my needs, and he cared for me. He saved my life because I would forget to eat.

The feeling of dependence is agonizing and so the mind tells you that you must start doing anything that you can do yourself. I thought to myself, "First heal that leg, because if the infection continues to pass through your bloodstream, it'll fuck up everything and it will kill you." You get gangrene throughout your whole body, a septicaemia, and then you die. Knowing this, I did everything possible to clear it out, and I would spend the time removing the pus from myself, and also from Numa.

We were both doing the same but we were getting weaker, because Numa also had trouble eating. He had also given much more of himself than me in every way, and, consequently, had expended much more energy – amongst other things by climbing up and down the mountains on previous expeditions.

While in that state, physically disabled by my gangrenous leg and having almost no power to move, I felt completely dependent on the others. That made me feel useless and caused me a lot of distress.

Despite that, I never complained. Yes, some nights I cried, but silently, and inwardly. You cried inwardly so that they wouldn't hear you, because it was contagious. It made me sad to hear someone crying. The real mercy for someone who is suffering is when you put yourself in their place and suffer with them.

From my stillness, I carefully observed the behaviour of others, each so different, but with a common denominator; to take care of one other. And they did so with me.

This led me to try to give something back somehow for all those caring acts, and I realized that humour was a great tool, and one that I could easily provide! To defuse conflicts and confront frustrations, to get smiles and even laughter in such a situation, seemed to be something that was crucially lacking. And when I saw them like that, laughing out loud, it gave me great satisfaction, and I felt better and mentally stronger. It would draw them away from their pain for a moment, and relieve some hysteria. It also made me feel useful because I could contribute something!

The mind dominates everything, and with those smiles, we would come out feeling relaxed and stronger. And it did me a lot of good personally, having my moment in the spotlight, and giving what was expected of me.

They also joked and made fun of me and my situation, and this alleviated my concerns, adding a farcical but jovial aspect to them.

Looking for a way out

We were already into November and, with eight friends killed in the avalanche, we somehow understood that this thing would continue, and for a long time. I had assumed that our ordeal would be long but not as prolonged as it turned out to be.

But once you perceive the presence of Jesus Christ, you find a certain peace. Because you saw men acting with love for one another in a way that seemed to mirror the image and likeness of God himself.

I noticed when the group suddenly changed, as if something new was motivating them, with a new attitude, a new determination, because they felt the presence of Jesus Christ. They began to make themselves heard, and to act in a different way. Some said spiritedly, "OK, let's get out of here, when shall we leave?" Others responded with just as much determination: "No, we should wait until the snow hardens, and the days are longer."

It was still terribly cold. Who was going to go? To the east or to the west? No, downwards... towards Argentina, to the east, which was easier.

Expeditions to here and to there. Tactics within a strategy of trial and error...

Three of us had shown in one of the expeditions that spending the night outdoors high in the mountains, at that time of year, might not kill you, but it would certainly leave you broken and weak. Gustavo had become almost blind, Daniel Maspons had stopped talking, and Numa had lost so much energy that his physical condition had deteriorated enormously.

There had been various expeditions. One day, they had gone off on a laborious trek and had come across the tail of the aircraft, which had ended up quite a distance away after splitting off in the crash. They had returned there another day with Roy Harley, who was a first-year engineering student, to see if he could fix the aircraft's radio in the hope of being able to transmit. It was an almost impossible task for Roy, because the unit was ruined and there were hundreds of detached cables. Nevertheless, he gave it every effort, and he also sacrificed himself. He expended all his energy to the extent that he almost died.

He spent several days trying to connect the radio batteries, not knowing that the effort was doomed to failure, and, already exhausted, he felt relieved when, finally, they all returned to his 'cottage', our home in the mountains.

Roy came back frail and as thin as a rake. They had spent about a week down there, and although it didn't turn out well in the end and Roy went from bad to worse, there is no doubt that he sacrificed himself for the others.

It was very similar to what happened to Numa.

By the end, the worst off were Roy and me, to the point where the others were making bets as to who would die first.

And so we started the process of deciding in which direction to set out.

We wanted to find the best way of doing that and our main driving force was to see our family and friends again – our most important bonds. This is the only thing that mattered to me and I'm sure everyone else felt the same. Because that group of men had turned into a formidable team, sharing a common objective, which was to return to their families. They used every available means, drawing on strength that they didn't possess; Nando to see his father, Roberto so that his mother wouldn't suffer. I wanted to return to see Soledad and my mum, whom I had left without the protection that I had planned to provide. What would become of them? That's why I wanted to return. The family was and is the most important thing. And so we made plans. "We will leave on such-and-such a day." "We will make a sleeping bag."

I helped with the sewing of the sleeping bag. And I contributed something.

But sometimes I didn't participate because they were all on the other side of the plane and it was quite difficult for me to move. I was very weak. I had got increasingly weak, quite apart from the wound. I spent a lot of time inside the plane with Numa and anyone else not going out. Roy also started to stay inside, and Fito would come in and help us, and would bring us water.

Fito remained in very good physical condition right up to the end. He had no problems eating, he would exercise, and he also went on some hikes. We, on the other hand, were deteriorating day by day.

The word 'parasite', which appears in the book *Alive* in reference to us, is a misnomer. A parasite is someone who lives off another and although I did nothing and the others took care of me, I was not a parasite. All I could do was talk, act as a calming influence, and brighten things up a little. As Roberto once said, "Everyone wanted to be around Coche."

I knew that laughing was a good remedy. I was sure of it. My father was a cheerful guy, and you wouldn't hear screaming or heated arguments in our house. It was harmonious and relaxed, with a lot of laughter. And so I tried to maintain that atmosphere up there.

That also happens in my current family... One day there was music playing (because Soledad always puts on music that she likes) and someone who came in said, "How peaceful it is here!" This with the children playing... I couldn't believe it!

The line

I stayed sound in mind despite the gangrene – 'lucid' is the word I'd use.

You had to control your anguish, because anguish causes pain. It's like breathing with your heart rather than your lungs. It hurts you and the pain eventually overrides your reason and your lucidity. I had realized that and I said to myself: 'If I'm in anguish, I won't be able to think properly.'

I had to stay very lucid to do everything for the others, just as they did for me... And in the end, lucidity also led me to the decision to die, when I wrote that I would die on 24th December. Because dying also seduced me. And it has continued to do so – that has never gone away.

The conflict was between life and death, on the boundary. On the line. You fell to one side or the other. This is a permanent conflict, being on that line. It is the conflict of being human.

I experienced it in an extreme form, and I know that there is meaning in both life and death.

They laughed at my situation – because I was a goner – speculating as to whether Roy or I would die first. It didn't bother me, but one day Roy got angry.

I read somewhere, and it is true, that anguish tightens your chest but not as if someone were pressing on it. It tightens your chest so that you have difficulty breathing, in addition to which we were high in the Andes, where the air was thin.

Your heart pushes against you and replaces your lucidity, and you want to cry and are not lucid and cannot think. There is a pill for this, such as Alprazolam, which comes with the promise, 'Take it and it will go away'. I once took a large one of these, and I felt happy and wanted more. And the psychiatrist told me, "No, it's addictive, like morphine." But up there we didn't have any pill!

Sometimes up there on the mountain you would hear loud laughter and political discussions interspersed by swearing. Because el Vasco[1] was right-wing and Arturito was left-wing. They were always very close together because they were good friends. I remember that they were always looking at a map, trying to locate Curicó, which the pilot had mentioned before he died. And we didn't know whether it was a mountain, a river or a village. "Look at this map," we had said, handing them a navigational chart, but the Chilean side was full of places and there was nothing on the Argentinian side. I remember looking for Curicó on that map. We thought that if we had passed Curicó, as the pilot had said before his death, then the green valleys of Chile would be behind the enormous mountain facing us...

That was why the expeditionaries headed west on the final trek.

Although, ultimately, it came down to what Nando said; the direction in which he wanted to go, other than north or south, of course. It was what Nando wanted. He was the one who had the willpower to set off. He was the only one, the only one! Who would go with him?

The fear that they would have setting off from there, the dread. I imagine that is why Roberto delayed the sewing of the sleeping bag, and tore it, and was bad-tempered. We always had to put up with his bad moods. The great fear that they would have, though that was not the case with Nando, who wanted to go much earlier. It was lucky that it happened that way, that they set off on 12th December, because it turned out to be the right day, never snowing once during their entire journey.

And Roberto set off anyway, despite his fear. Courage is born of deep fear. Roberto had a deep-seated fear just as I would have had. Courage is thinking, 'I'm afraid but this is what I have to do. It doesn't make much difference whether we die sitting facing each other in the fuselage or I die walking with Nando.'

Numa died on 11th December, the birthday of both Gastón and Javier, and that sad event triggered the departure of the three expeditionaries, which took place the following day.

---

[1] 'the Basque', nickname of Rafael Echavarren

The last fifty-six days

Numa deserved a prize for his effort, for giving and giving of himself to those who needed it most, attending to everyone, overcoming fatigue, and forcing his body to suffer a little more. But the prize for virtue is in virtue itself. Numa was a good man to his core! And he never tired of being so…

From that moment, I have felt that death is not a punishment, as it is typically considered to be here on Earth (the death penalty); rather, in very special circumstances, it is peace. And when we die, those who suffer are those who love us and who remain living in this world, without thinking that the soul of the person that died is in a paradise of peace and happiness. Life ends, but not existence. Existence is eternal, like the mountains.

Why was I still alive? I was saved when the aeroplane crashed into the mountain, due to where I had been sitting. Gastón had called out to me to sit down next to him in the back row but just at that moment someone else sat down in my place, and I went forward past the wing, and sat on the left, next to the skinny Menéndez, whom I had just met. I didn't die of cold on the first night, because human warmth had prevented that. I had changed places with our team captain Marcelo at his request and he died in the avalanche in my place, while I was saved in his. And finally, just two days before Christmas Eve, 24th December, the day on which I had already decided to die, Nando came looking for us with two helicopters, having crossed the Andes with Roberto Canessa, walking, scrambling, climbing, and suffering the most hostile and inhospitable conditions over ten days.

And he located us in that immensity…

Daily routine

This is a depiction of what we did day after day. Monotony, conserving energy... and making water. Such an important task!!

There is a boy without a shirt, so it must be December.

You can see the radio by the side of the person lying in the foreground. It was our only connection with the world of men.

To hear those well-known jingles so close to Christmas would make us very sad and we would switch it off!

chapter V Memories

Three sweets

I think that when you perform a good deed for someone, something good will sooner or later come your way in return. That's what happened to me with Liliana Navarro de Methol: a woman with whom everyone got along; who had made sure that the small amount of water we were able to make in October was distributed equitably; who refused any privilege she might have claimed as a member of the so-called 'weaker sex', and who displayed such strength of character, and had so many other qualities that the young men of this earth often lack. Yes, she accepted the toilet that we had made to protect her privacy. And, after several refusals, she agreed to swap places with me one night. I made the offer because the place where she slept was horrible, and I was feeling quite well. So I spent almost the whole night on my feet, because I couldn't lie down or even sit. Resting my head on my arms, supported by the rack above the seats, I slept standing up, like a horse. And poking around in the rack during that silent, dark, and terribly cold night, I found three dulce de leche caramels.

My first impulse was to follow the existing rules, which obliged me to share them with the others, but it was easy to see that everyone would only get a single lick. I told myself that my discovery must be the result of the good deed that I'd done for Liliana and so because that concerned me and me alone, the sweets were mine.

I think that I must have taken about an hour with each sweet. First, the process of unwrapping it – I did that very slowly so that nobody would hear the wrapper crinkling. Then, after licking the sweet, I popped it into my mouth, which I kept well-closed so that nothing would be lost or heard. And then I slowly savoured the sweet, and felt the joy of it trickling down to my wasted stomach. I repeated the process with the second sweet and I thought about saving the third, but as no one had noticed, I ate it without leaving any trace. I felt so good!

Making Water

Here!

Fito's hand bringing the best gift – a full bottle of water just for me. It is because of actions such as this and many others that I didn't die.

The Rosary

Carlitos was our expert when it came to the Rosary. He made us pray every day, and you either considered God a friend, or were very angry with Him. Because more than once, and after repeated frustrations, the anger would surface, and it was aimed at this god who was responsible for so much suffering.

We asked Him what we had done to deserve such punishment. Because, believe me, it was much harder and more painful than anything portrayed in any book or film.

One or other of the various books written by my companions might present a harsher or more detailed picture than another but to my mind, it was much worse than anything you could possibly know. In those seventy-two days, we were the most impoverished people in the world; the most dispossessed, the forgotten, given up for dead. We endured the thirst and the cold, we ate from the flesh of our friends, humiliated to the depth of the abyss. Continuously over the seventy-two days, in body, mind, and soul. And with no end in sight!

But praying helped to calm us. It was as if we were speaking with God and He was speaking with us when we prayed our Salve Regina.

A Dying Companion

It is heartbreaking to remember this image!

The notebook

But not everything was a dead loss. I stayed alive and I wrote, in a notebook that I had found, everything that I would do if I were to be rescued. I would return to my house in Montevideo. I would camp out near the kitchen and refrigerator so that I could open it whenever I wanted. I would lie down in my bed and would have light blue pyjamas with bright blue trim, and a soft pillow. I would call my mother and Soledad and they would care for my every need. I would later marry Soledad and form a family, my own family, and I would go to live on the dairy farm in Puntas de Maciel, Florida. I would have my children, and would try to convey all the revelations and understandings that I had received during my seventy-two days on the mountain. That everything can be lost in an instant, and that everything remains with you as a legacy of the soul, which is an immeasurable force, and which also gives you the will to live even in the presence of suffering. And when that suffering ends, the legacy that remains with you, and its values, make you a complete man and take you down the path of happiness to peace, which is what we all seek.

I think that the future I wrote about in that notebook (which I still possess) has already been realized. I have lived it and enjoyed it. Not without setbacks, not without often letting myself get caught up in earthly and material things, but it has always resurfaced. The only thing that I didn't write about, and which has now been given to me as a gift, was the incredible pleasure of being a grandfather! And I want to share this with everyone, what I've strived for in life, and I think it has served well, because my three children are proof of it in their daily lives, in their families, their friends, and their jobs. They are the children that I dreamed of having, but better still! And to be their father makes me proud.

All this would have been impossible without my sweet companion Soledad, who is now referred to as Grandma Buba by the grandchildren. She has always accompanied me with love, patience and intelligence. I think that she is the best present that life has given me, and after forty-seven years of marriage, she is still by my side. Together, we did everything, had everything, and passed everything on. It is about values, but truly human values, unlike those held by some societies, or individuals in certain societies, for whom the only value is power

Among ourselves

Daniel Fernández, to this very day, has at his disposal a 'slave', Bobby François, who swore to be so for life in gratitude for all the care that he received.

Also, it was moving to see the way in which the boys tended to el Vasco and Arturo. The love with which they fed them and took care of their injuries!

Alvarito, with his broken leg, never requested any help; he dragged himself through the snow with his hands and came out to work every day, making water or sewing the sleeping bags.

And Carlitos, after having once heard me sing the *Marcha de Tres Árboles* (a hymn of the Partido Nacional, my political party), took charge of my injured leg, taking care of it up to the very last day!

Certainly, there were situations that bothered me and got me riled. Daniel took care of his precious shoes as if they were a national treasure. At night, he would take them off and put them on the luggage shelf above, joined together and in order, and I thought, 'That arsehole, where on earth does he think we are?'

On four occasions, we used pieces of wood from a Coca-Cola crate to make a fire, and we were then able to cook the meat on a sheet of aluminium. It was when I was recovering, because I was with the Strauch cousins and I was scrounging freely. Eduardo would refuse my pleas, because he said that cooking the meat reduced it, which was true, but it was also undeniable that, cooked, it was easier to eat, and I could then ingest more. Eduardo's refusal made me want to strangle him, but the day arrived when the wood was finished and no one would give you a dollar bill to light a fire.

When a suitcase full of cigarettes appeared and they began being distributed, Pedro's turn arrived and a second before he said, "I don't smoke," I told him, "Say yes, and keep them for me." When I went to claim them, he said to me, "And what are you going to give me in exchange?" I offered him dollars... No! Eventually he agreed to part of my daily ration. And in his book, he says that he did everything to integrate himself into the group... Anyway, due to the reserve of cigarettes that Pedro amassed, it was possible for me to smoke almost without restriction.

One night, Numa got angry with Tintín for some reason I don't remember but seeing Numa provoked to such anger infuriated me also and, speaking across the pitch-black darkness, I challenged Tintín to fight us in a duel the next morning. Nothing happened and Tintín was saved from a beating. Anything negative was quickly forgotten.

Liliana

Liliana merits a few special lines from me. She was the only woman who survived the accident. She exercised her protective and caring instinct, common to many woman, as if we were her own four children. Her face transmitting love and her behaviour demonstrating it... all of us enjoyed being with her, just like chicks with the mother hen. She taught us to care, to give, and to give ourselves. She was fair, and brave, and spirited. After she died in the avalanche, I saw my companions behave towards those most in need in a way that mirrored and resembled her. This made them more feminine, but more complete as men.

Every man has a feminine side – the anima in Jungian psychology. Up there, the moment came at which circumstances led us to reveal our feminine side, expressed as protection, care, and love for the others.

Mary was also present up there!

I remember Javier going every day to the place where Liliana's corpse lay – he would kneel and speak to her. It would weigh heavy on my heart, and I felt so sad that I tried not to look. Thirty years later, in one of our frequent reunions, Javier told us that one day he went out to perform the ritual with her, and did not find her. He thought that her body had been used for food, and he had borne that belief without sharing it. We had agreed that the bodies of Nando's mother and sister would be the last ones we would turn to, and we had placed Liliana next to them with the same idea. And so we told this to Javier.

I can still see the smiles and tears of joy on Javier's face!

The final expedition

The day of the final expedition arrived: 12th December 1972. A month and a half of preparation and logistics, in which the three chosen expeditionaries ate at will whatever they liked. They did not rotate at night, they slept in the best places; the ones that they chose, and they took the best clothes. Each one was given a full backpack, stocked for a week of hiking, of which Tintín's appeared to be the heaviest. The rest of us followed the general rules, the small daily ration, rotation at night, and no complaints about the bad mood of an expeditionary.

They left very early, heading west, to climb the huge wall that surrounded us like a horseshoe. They made a direct assault on it, because we didn't know any better.

They didn't want to head east, because they said that there was a huge mountain blocking the way. I and some others insisted that there would be exits to either side of that mountain (Sosneado). It was all downhill and so would be much easier to traverse.

Memories

But to the west was Chile, and we dreamt about its green valleys. The expeditionaries finally decided this was the way to go, based on the erroneous information that the pilot had given us before he died, saying that we had passed Curicó.

During the farewell, there were personal conversations that I don't remember, and anecdotes such as that of the little shoes that I also don't recall, but which feature in the book *Alive*. My only thought on seeing them head off was: 'There goes my life.' In those legs and in that will that would compel them to carry on even when they wanted to give up.

I was prostrate, without hunger, without the will to keep on fighting to live, and I was approaching the end.

I watched them all day, as they were slowly climbing, and suffering in the attempt. I thought of them at night, packed tight in their three-person sleeping bag, and I saw that the nights were clear and moonlit, but higher up they would have to contend with wind and terrible cold. I saw the summit that they had to reach without imagining that it was only the first of several.

The next morning, 13th December 1972, two months after the accident, we were finally making a serious attempt to escape from our prison.

I went out of the fuselage early and it took a while for me to locate our expeditionaries. You could see three small figures, which didn't seem to move, but they appeared smaller than the previous day. They were making progress... and I stayed watching them all day.

After another night; longer but not as cold, I woke up again. I was soon outside, looking for those three little figures, which I located in that white and black immensity. Then I lost sight of them, and I imagined that they had reached the summit and would be looking down on those green Chilean valleys of our dreams!

I don't know quite when, but someone alerted us that one of the three was coming down at great speed. And indeed, it appeared that a small figure was descending rapidly towards us. It took an hour for him to reach a height at which we could recognize whom it was. It was Tintín and I thought the worst. The other two would have died, since there were many ways in which that could have happened. Many more ways to die than to survive and ultimately succeed.

Tintín, seeing the anguish reflected in our faces, immediately reassured us: "They decided to continue by themselves. It will take longer than we thought and calculated; so I left them my backpack and returned here."

My heart swelled with relief. The expedition had not been aborted! I felt more and more grateful towards them. Tintín returned to join the group and he immediately lost all the privileges of the expeditionaries.

But that was the start for me of the seven most distressing days of waiting – would it be success or failure?

Success was to return home; failure was to die after having endured so much suffering. A thin line, one that I no longer had any control over, separated life and death, and this time there would not be one more day, a new dawn, a hope... or perhaps there would! My life was in the hands of Nando and Roberto, and our last vestiges of hope, already endangered and starting to slip away, rested in those two men. Hope is the dream of a man awake, and I was already sleeping... without major conflicts... and at peace!

I saw myself, as in a mirror, in the faces of the others; haggard, eyes sunk to the depths of their sockets, a sharp aquiline nose, cracked and bleeding lips, skin dark and greenish, and hair a tangle of neglect.

I was most reminded of my previous life at night-time, when I wouldn't be looking at the high mountains that surrounded us, and I would think a lot about my family and my friends. But now I thought of Nando and Roberto, who were walking in search of their salvation and ours.

Our lives depended on the success of the mission, which relied not only on their will and courage, but also on their faith to move mountains.

I thought that God was with them, and He would show them the way into that vastness. Because they gave everything, everything they had, and I hoped that God would provide the rest.

I thought about my family, Soledad, and my friends; those who were still with me, those who had died, and my friends in Uruguay, who would be well. I had wanted to tell them that I loved them and missed them. Now I also wanted to tell them what I felt, the new meaning of life, to share it with them. To let them know that I had discovered many important things that Jesus, the man, had revealed. He had shown me the way, expressing himself through my friends. And I would tell them everything so that they would have no need to suffer. How I loved and missed them!

Godspeed!

Thirteen bidding farewells to three. It was on 12th December 1972

And descending into a sort of lethargy, immersed in my thoughts, I wrote in my notebook that if Roberto and Nando hadn't arrived by 22nd December, ten days after setting off, I would give myself two more days, until 24th December 1972, Christmas Eve, and then I would succumb and go in search of my father, Gastón, and the others, to where I knew they dwelt. I would not struggle to live any longer. Death was the alternative that had begun to seduce me... and it made sense!

chapter VI **Being reborn**

22nd December

By 22nd December, the fuselage was no longer buried, and so we didn't have to crawl in and out like rodents any more. The sun on those long, hot days had melted the snow that had covered the fuselage, which was now resting on a pedestal of ice maintained by its own shadow.

It took quite a bit of effort to enter, but you only had to jump down to exit.

Already weak, and with just sufficient strength to breathe quietly, I would stay inside most of the day, counting the days that remained. For the first time, I believed I knew the date that everything would end. Before, there had just been uncertainty. But now I had taken the decision to let myself die on Christmas Eve.

I went to sleep on the night of 21st December struggling hard to not give up hope. I thought about how much had happened since 13th October, and how little time remained until 24th December! But I knew that soon I would no longer be suffering. I had lost the necessary balance between body, soul and mind.

We were sleeping later now that the nights were not so cold. That morning, I was sitting alongside Fito, Carlitos, and others I don't remember. Something that morning told me that it was the date of the death of my grandfather, Nicolás Inciarte, the first of our family to arrive in Uruguay. I never knew him, nor did I generally remember the date, if I had ever heard it, yet that morning I had the certainty that he had died on that day.

Almost at the same time, Juvenal (Daniel Fernandez) appeared in the opening at the back, grabbed the curved walls of the fuselage with both hands, visible just from the waist upwards, and, with a face that I will never forget, smiling and with bigger eyes than ever, shouted, or rather howled, "Nando and Muscles have appeared! They made it! And now the helicopters are coming for us!"

Being reborn

It was as if my chest caught fire. An onrush of heat, of fire, of breathlessness... I don't know what it was... flooded my soul! My mind then assimilated what it had heard, that thunderbolt that had made my heart palpitate at high speed by pumping more blood than my lungs could process. I was choking, trying to breathe and shout at the same time. I couldn't speak because of the emotion!

Those of us who were inside hugged each other, we couldn't find the words! I think that the only reason the fuselage didn't roll down the slope below was that Daniel was holding it with his arms. We slowly made our way out, jumping down onto the ice of the glacier, which now no longer had a covering of snow. Because it hadn't snowed at all during those ten days. The glacier gives rise to the river that runs due east, emanating from the high valley where we were living. It is called the Valley of Tears, which is mentioned many times in the Rosary prayer: "To you do we send up our sighs, mourning and weeping in this valley of tears..." Though it was rare that anybody cried and, when they did, nobody saw it.

We washed our faces and hair for the first time. There was plenty of water stored in an oddly-shaped steel trashcan.

We exchanged clothes, returning each item, which someone had made good use of over the seventy-two days, to its original owner. The sense of ownership re-emerged at the prospect of returning to our previous life!

We broke several combs trying to untangle our matted hair and by around 6:30 a.m. we were already sitting, almost clean, almost well-dressed and presentable, peering into the sky, looking for the promised helicopters. But the hours passed and no one appeared and then I wondered whether it might have all been an illusion and none of this had happened.

Then at around 1:00 p.m. we heard a distant *tac-tac-tac*, coming from the west, and carried by the wind, because at that time of day there was strong and unpredictable turbulence. We stayed on our feet, straining our necks as we looked expectantly up into the sky above. After many, many minutes, someone shouted, from the depth of his being, "THERE, THEY'RE COMING FROM OVER THERE!" and pointed downward, towards the east, towards the valley. Nothing was coming from the sky above; they were coming from below! Two black dots, in silence, broke the monotony of the landscape that we knew so well! They were moving relative to our fixed references, and in a few moments there were two helicopters flying over us in circles, with a din that put an end to our usual silence. The swirling blades were causing the snow to fly in every direction and we were waving with our arms upraised so that the scene resembled more an exotic dance than a rescue.

The sound of the helicopters was music! The engines sounded like the melody to *Ode to Joy*.

Later my mother told me, "It was as if you were born again," and I think that from 6:30 a.m. to 1:00 p.m. the wait was like childbirth, bringing suffering, but then life. It was as if I were seeing my own birth, being born from the heart of the Andes, emerging into life via the helicopters.

Hours earlier, when Daniel had given the news that he had heard on the radio, I had started to doubt that it was true. That most welcome news could have been a hallucination, like the time someone had wanted to go out at night and buy Coca-Cola and pizza, and someone else had requested, "With mozzarella!" And as eight, nine, ten o'clock had passed by already and nothing was appearing in the sky, I doubted the veracity of the radio listeners. I gave them credit in the end, because it turned out well for me.

The flight

I was sitting in the snow, exhausted by emotion, and suddenly two men in red parkas jumped out of a helicopter that was hovering close to the ground. As those who could ran to those aircraft, one of those rescuers, whom I had so often dreamed of, lifted me up in his arms. He threw me up, and a white-helmeted crew member motioned to me to grab his arms. I hit hard against the edge of the floor, hurting myself, and he pulled me towards the centre of the cabin and sat me in a seat against the back wall. Excited, I grabbed his helmet to hug him and kiss him, and the guy pushed me back against the seat and fastened my seatbelt. Who will believe my intentions? He was the first terrestrial person I encountered, whom I was hugging in an expression of my happiness, perhaps rather excessively for his liking.

I thought that everyone was on board. I don't remember who was in my helicopter H89. But I certainly recall vividly the vibration of the helicopter and the roar of the engines, just as in the aeroplane before the crash. We were moving from side to side at the mercy of the winds, which were chaotically shaking the two helicopters that were crossing each other's paths and approaching dangerously close to those black rocks. My joy was tinged with terror, and I asked myself, "Why on earth did I get on board this machine which is about to crash?" It was like on one of those street-corners of Montevideo in autumn (I am imagining one in the Aguada district), where the fallen leaves of the banana trees are lifted by the winds meeting at the crossroads and fly around madly, without rhyme or reason.

Helicopters (Drawing)

Helicopters (Painting)

Just as in the plane before the crash, I closed my eyes and awaited another explosion. Suddenly, there was absolute silence, and I wondered if everything had already ended and I was dead, once again at the end of the road.

But the helicopter was gliding on a hot air current and ascending (as described in the subsequent report of Commander Jorge Massa), without the roar of its engines, to exit the Valley of Tears. I opened my eyes, anxious to see the reality, the truth of it, and I could see that I was still in the aircraft, and through the window I could make out on the snow, the shape of the fuselage already far off, already small and distant...

As I was moving away from the place, the fuselage and its surroundings were becoming smaller, and I felt that I was leaving behind something of mine, uniquely mine, that had been experienced, seen, and felt; something that already would never happen again, and I realized that I was leaving behind a part of myself. Today, I think I have something from there inside me, that will never leave me.

Goodbyes

The living and the dead, saying goodbye to each other.

Suitcases with their belongings for their families.

And God, with headphones, guiding the helicopters, and showing the way as always, to whoever wants to open his soul to Him.

Before it disappeared from my view, I thought of everything that I had left behind in that place; my dead friends who would live with me always, suffering, pain, anxiety, anguish, despair, and the most atrocious humiliation; the collapse of the human into the worst condition, carried into the darkest depths of an unknown void.

But I wasn't just leaving that place, and ending something terrible. I was also bringing out with me something that I felt, that I knew, that had been revealed to me for the first time; that I had seen with my own eyes and had internalized in mind, body and soul. It was like a secret treasure which someday I would have to share, too important for me to keep under lock and key. It took thirty years to do so.

I had felt the presence of God, and had known him through men, through my friends. It was in their looks; in their actions; in their words; in the courage that they showed, that arises out of the most absolute fear, and overcomes it; and in their great love towards each other. It is not worth saving yourself if you do not leave or do something for someone else; something that serves him; something that helps him. Love is not only about feeling, but is principally about behaviour. Love is the most intelligent thing. Intelligence and love are inseparable. Life consists of doing things, of working, but if you think about it, it deserves to be lived if we can share the good that we have with someone else, and if that person repeats it to another, and so on. That is the meaning of life for me!

Los Maitenes

Soon, we land in a beautiful place; green, with trees, life, colours, and flowing water. And people run to help you, to treat you and save you... and, even though they don't know you, it seems that they love you and that you are someone very important for them. And you again get that feeling of not being worthy to receive so much from so many!

The place is called Los Maitenes – named after a native Chilean tree, because we were in Chile, in the green Chilean valley of our dreams!

A soldier offered me cigarettes and I offered him some of mine from those that I had left. Our needs manifested through a common language.

I realized that not all my friends were there. I saw Daniel, Alvaro, Pedro, Carlitos, and Eduardo; and Nando the great, the magnificent, the unwavering, who pushed, urged, and stretched himself to the limit to save all of us. Great, all of them great! Each in his own way. "If you can't be a pine on the top of the hill, be a scrub in the valley – but be. If you can't be a bush, be a bit of the grass. If you can't be a highway, be a trail. If you can't be the sun, be a star. It isn't by size that you win or you fail. BE THE BEST OF WHATEVER YOU ARE!"[2]. And each one was that for me: the best of whatever they were. Whatever your role is, whatever you are or whatever you do, bring to bear all the strength of your feelings and your heart. How to acknowledge all this?

We ate and drank whatever they gave us. A military nurse, named Koch, undertook the initial treatment of my gangrenous leg – which wouldn't stop oozing pus – with professionalism and care, and even a smile.

And I continued receiving love through many treatments. This also forms part of our human condition, of our species, and once again I felt proud to belong to it.

I had thought that the other eight would arrive soon, but later I heard that they would be rescued early the next morning, as it was impossible to fly over the place that afternoon. It was too dangerous, and we had only been able to leave thanks to the expertise and courage of Commanders Massa and Garcia and the heroic crew.

Here, I give all my appreciation and thanks to the Chilean Air Force. Because I didn't yet know of the existence of Sergio Catalán; the first man, the first human instrument, that came to the aid of two ragged Uruguayans he didn't know. He rode many hours to alert the authorities. He rescued them, and he gave them food. The solidarity of simple country-folk; the giving over of his time; his intelligence to realize what he was dealing with. He was one more factor in a chain of men and events which were indispensable in our coming out alive at the end. When it comes to exalting mankind, Sergio Catalán is a prime example.

---

[2] Excerpt from *Be the Best of Whatever You Are* by Douglas Malloch

Los Maitenes

In Los Maitenes, treading on grass and being attended to by unknown people, but it seemed that they loved me and I didn't know why. What had I done?

Green Valley

The Chilean valley that we all dreamt of. It was real!

Soledad

More than two months had passed since the accident; two months in which my world had changed substantially. The joy, the hope, the thousand and one projects, had disappeared from my life. Occasionally, a tiny glimmer of hope still appeared, but its force was so faint and so fleeting that as soon as I thought I saw it, it had already disappeared.

I had fallen into a deep, dark well, in which my waking up each morning was my nightmare. I couldn't face that new day, generally warm and bright in December, with all its hustle and bustle, the people in the street and the Christmas jingles. I didn't understand how the world could continue on its way without Coche and my other friends. I saw happy people, and I longed for the past, for times that could never return. That farewell from the aeroplane steps was already far, far away, and whenever I thought about it, which was almost constantly, the pain and anguish were so strong that they didn't allow me to think, to act, to live…

My family spent those two and a half months sticking close to me. I felt that they were suffering just as much as me, and they tried to surround me, to take care of me, and to avoid leaving me alone in my terrible suffering.

My mother was like my shadow, always accompanying me, willing to take me to and from the house of the radio hams, the airport, the church, and all the meetings where we were deciding what steps to take next. She cried with me a lot, and in her embrace, support, and company I found some of the self-control and protection to withstand everything that I was going through.

My father, uncharacteristically, did not lose hope. He was always lifting my spirits. He told me that it was not all said and done, that no evidence of a wrecked plane had ever appeared, nor any remains that would allow us to conclude a tragic end. That I should wait, that they could still appear. And I answered him, incredulously, that this only happened in the movies, not in real life, to which he responded, "What is cinema, if not an imitation of real life?" and that "Everything is possible." That optimistic attitude of my father, which I much admired, not only surprised me but also made me smile. In those two long months, he moved his office to our home, to be closer to me and to any news. Secretaries and stenographers came, but he didn't set foot in his study. Also during that period, he lost fourteen kilos. He suffered a lot, watching me suffer, and that suffering extended to all of us… to my sister and brother, who were just kids then.

My sister had her fourteenth birthday on the day following the accident. But there was no joy for her on that day, no friends, no gifts, no candles… I remember her today, always present, accompanying me with her silence and her eyes full of tenderness, affection, and compassion.

My brother was ten years old then and he had been distraught. Not only was he a student of the Christian Brothers, and so was experiencing everything in a particularly close-up and special way, but he adored Coche, and could not understand what had happened, and it was hard for him to adapt to the atmosphere in the house. Coche had been teaching him to play chess, and so they would spend a lot of time together. He never wanted to play anymore...

To this day, more than forty years later, I know and feel how this story has marked them. And I thank them for what, at their age and in their own way, they knew to give me.

It was the evening of Thursday 21st December when I went to answer the phone. This time it was another Rosina who was calling; Rosina Urioste de Strauch, the mother of Fito, a good friend of Coche who was also missing.

It is very difficult today, aged sixty-five, to recall her exact words, or the feelings that they immediately generated in me. The uncertainty, the fear, and the anxiety all returned in full force.

Two guys had thrown a message, attached to a stone, across the Tinguiririca River in Chile, to a local herdsman. The message said that they were Uruguayans!

With that call, all my vital signs sprang to life again...

Could it be possible this time? I didn't want to admit to myself or imagine what this could mean...

So many false alarms had given us hope over the course of those seventy long days! Just to have those hopes dashed. Only the voice of Carlitos Páez Vilaró via the radio, and the continuing presence of Rafael Ponce de León with his communications, had been a constant light during those long dark nights of October, November and December 1972.

And then Friday 22nd December arrived.

In the early hours of the morning, we learnt the names of the two boys who had crossed the cordillera on foot, defying the impossible. Nando Parrado and Roberto Canessa. From that point on, those two names would be inexorably linked to the greatest joy of my life. All my gratitude goes to them, today, and always, and eternally!

I hadn't yet been able to sleep that night, with the radio and phones flooded with the news, which was always the same, repeated a thousand times; there were sixteen survivors, but twenty-nine had died... The latter figure was overwhelming to me, and to all of us. And they couldn't know the names until the helicopters reached the scene of the accident to rescue the remaining fourteen, in case any more might have died during Roberto and Nando's ten-day hike.

It is impossible to describe those hours of waiting on that warm morning of Friday 22nd December.

It was hell inside me; it was horror; it was panic; it was immense pain, in anticipation of what I knew would come. I sought peace, I sought answers, but no one could give them to me. We just embraced our family, and our friends, and in those embraces we found a bit of solace, and less loneliness.

And so the morning passed... some were already flying to Chile with tears of joy, others flying without knowing what they were going to find; everyone searching for the truth about what happened, even if that truth might be hard to face. I admired their courage... When would this agony end? My mind could no longer think, my lucidity had escaped me, I was not physically able to stand up anymore, and my breathing was short and hurried, interrupted every now and then by a deeper breath to revive myself.

But everything has its end, or its transformation, and it was around 2 o'clock on the afternoon of 22nd December when the agonizing uncertainty ended. For some it began once again, that deep pain, which I can't even imagine; for others, the joy and the disbelief in the resurrection of their loved one, but an incomplete joy, because of so many friends lost; so many of their families suffering; families with whom we had shared everything during those two long months.

There was a crowd on Puyol Street, and Ponce de Leon's garden and the pavement outside his house were crammed with people. There, his ham radio was transmitting the news. Cars were parked throughout the entire block, and beyond. Mobile recording vans from various TV stations were trying to communicate what was happening. But everything turned to silence, overwhelming silence, when the loudspeakers began to announce, one by one, the names of those who had survived the tragedy.

Standing on the sidewalk, surrounded by people, and holding the hands of several friends, I waited for his name, that of Coche... 'José Luis Iriarte'. That had to be Inciarte... I knew that there was no Iriarte.

They named him, he was the fourteenth... just two remained. An interminable and heart-rending list, but at the same time, very short.

Someone held me up because I felt that I was going to fall. I couldn't believe it... I was defending a delusion! And I went into the house, making my way through that crowd, my soul flooded with tears, almost unable to breathe, wanting to confirm what I had just heard. Coche was alive? Was it true?

The very narrow staircase going down to radio room was packed with people of all ages, on every step all the way down. It was impossible to get through! I couldn't reach Rafael and so I shouted out his name. Then he turned around, his back to the radio, and looked up to see who was calling him... and he saw me... and smiled... and raised his thumb...

That already said everything.

Ever since, I have always carried this memory with me.

Coche was alive! It was true!

Even today, forty years later, I can hardly believe everything that happened, and that happened to me.

I feel that I have a debt with God, and with life.

I am also eternally grateful to everyone who made it possible for Coche to survive and so allow us to form this wonderful family of ours.

And I have never forgotten any of those dear friends who remained on the mountain. To them especially, all my gratitude.

May God bless us all!

The reunion

From Los Maitenes, we set off once again in a helicopter, flying to the army base in the city of San Fernando. There they undressed me and I saw my very swollen knees. I couldn't imagine what had happened to them. Someone told me that all my thigh and calf muscle had disappeared, and so my knees stood out from my long leg bones. I didn't even know that I had lost forty-five kilos.

There, we were greeted by the dear Carlos Páez Vilaró, father of Carlitos, who, as everyone found out later, had been searching for us over those two months, and the Uruguayan Ambassador in Chile, César Charlone. There were also parents waiting for children who would not be returning.

Memories of the Andes

They put me on a stretcher, undressed and covered by a blanket, and took me in an ambulance to San Juan de Dios hospital in San Fernando. I remember a tunnel of male and female nurses all dressed in white, greeting me and stretching out their hands towards me. I gave them mine, but the blanket covering me almost slipped off and I had to withdraw my hand to secure that blanket covering my nakedness and dirtiness, my skeletal body, which my remaining or reborn modesty wanted to hide.

They put me in Room 1. I think that I'd never seen anything quite so lovely, so clean and so beautifully presented. It had a bed, mattress, pillow, and very white sheets. One wall was papered with flowers, and the other three painted with great care. A door and a tall window with curtains matching the wallpaper allowed me to see a beautiful garden full of colours, which was later invaded by cameramen, who were looking through my window, along with some nuns, who waved.

Shortly afterwards, on that same 22nd December, Dr Ausin entered the room. He checked me over, and while he was treating the wound to my right ankle, he casually asked me what I had last eaten. I thought about saying, "Chocolate," which the soldier at Los Maitenes had given me, and which I had devoured. But I understood that he was referring to the food during the seventy-two days, and I decided to tell him, and said, just as casually, "Human flesh." Dr Ausin continued with his task, as if nothing had been said. But when I was visiting San Fernando years later, he told me that he had almost fainted at my response.

I thought I would sleep peacefully that night, but I couldn't help hearing Carlitos' loud voice raised to maximum volume. We all reacted differently. Some, more excited than others, were talking non-stop; others of us were so overcome that we could hardly speak.

We were hungry and they were giving us only jelly! So some of my friends raided the kitchen that night and then, because I was attached to a drip dispensing various serums, they came over to my bed and we ate a great variety of stolen delights. The next morning, there was a great to-do among the hospital staff. They had noticed the theft, and the tell-tale signs lay on my bed.

A skinny young man dressed in Catholic clergy clothes also appeared in my room. His name was Andres Rojas and just seeing him, and the aura of peace that he imparted, led me to tell him everything that we had experienced, without exception, in a few minutes, with all the mysticism that filled my soul. After listening to me with much empathy, he told me that he was going to fetch the Eucharist and would return immediately. I asked whether I should confess before taking Communion, to which he responded that I already done so.

Being reborn

While I waited for him, I heard a loud voice shouting, "Inciarte, Algorta! Where are they?" I desperately tried to call out to him, because I recognized the voice as that of my uncle Carlos Algorta, also Pedro's uncle. But my voice sounded very low, weak, and barely audible...

He shot into my room like a waterspout. He was the first whom I saw of my longed-for family! Behind him came my older brother, Pololo, who, with eyes like hard-boiled eggs, was trying his hardest to recognize me.

Between the hugging, the crying, and the sobbing, they were shouting, and I wanted to respond to them but I still couldn't catch my breath, I could only whisper that I was full of God! And I was! We hugged at length, and in between fits of crying I spent the rest of the time just looking at them with glistening eyes, with all the love that I felt for them at that moment, and which I still feel today.

The next day, 23rd December, they took me to Santiago in an ambulance. My brother came with me, sitting beside my stretcher. We talked about everything, and he asked me, innocently I think, what we had eaten during those seventy-two days on the mountain. When I told him the truth, he said, "Yes, obviously," and immediately went as white as paper, and broke down. When the hospital staff in Santiago opened the ambulance door, they hesitated about which of the two of us they should attend to first!

I was in the intensive care unit of the Posta Central hospital in Santiago. Roy, who was very weak, was in the bed facing me. Alvarito was beside him, and Javier was next to me.

Suddenly, my mother entered. She looked at the four of us all lying in bed, and couldn't recognize me. All of us looked the same to her: beards, long hair, sunburnt faces and chapped lips, as well as our skeletal bodies. I had to call out for her to identify me. She was one of the reasons I had survived and endured everything. I don't remember much about our meeting, because the crying takes up all my memory.

I told her who the others were, and she greeted them one by one, thanking them for what they had done for me. I could not stop looking at her, she was so lovely! Her tenderness enveloped and comforted me. When the doctor said that she should leave, I didn't want to release her hand, but she told me, "Soledad is waiting to come in."

Soledad and my mother

As with my mother, Soledad was only able to recognize me by my calling out to her. She was also so beautiful, so clean, so full of light and love, and we embraced for a long time, sobbing so much that we couldn't utter a single word. But the doctor, seeing that I was crying a lot, separated us so as to prevent all those tears from doing me harm. I asked her to not forget to come and see me the next day, and she smiled as though she couldn't quite believe what I was saying. The next day it would be Christmas Eve! And I was going to continue living!

That night, a nurse passed by with a cake of strawberries and whipped cream, just like the one we had seen in a photo that had been passed around the fuselage. She refused to give us any, by order of the doctor, but in the end, she gave in to our pleas, and we experienced the taste of that cake from the photo we had all seen!

Roy and Javier were beset by a terrible diarrhoea and Alvarito and I were crying out for them to move room, the smell was so disgusting. We were slowly beginning to become civilized people.

Javier recovered, but Roy was completely dehydrated and had to be hospitalized at the clinic for several days, in a serious condition. Later, he returned to his former strength, fit and strong as a bull up to this day!

Being reborn

Alvarito was limping, but his leg had fused together almost perfectly. It only remained a little bit short. And all thanks to Roberto Canessa, who set it in those first few days, when he could only draw on the knowledge from his first year of medical school.

Javier walked out of the intensive care unit, as if it were nothing, to look for his four children and his brothers and sister. They were sure of Javier's survival, because in the past he had overcome some very serious situations in various accidents and had always pulled through: with a missing eye, a deaf ear and a metal plate in his head, but always alive.

Finally, Javier, who was the oldest of us all, died on 4th June 2015, after forty-two years of being part of the group of sixteen survivors.

chapter VII Returning

They discharged me from hospital on the morning of Sunday 24th December 1972. I got dressed in the clothes that they'd given me in San Fernando and, seeing myself in the mirror, I thought that I was the best-dressed man in the world. They had given me a bath; my first since October, and the water had instantly turned black. And it wasn't until the third rinse that I stopped losing the accumulated filth that was clinging to my body. Once the water cleared, my modesty resurfaced with the nurse present, but she didn't seem to care much about the human wretch in front of her. How good I felt and smelt! They weighed me and the scale showed forty-five kilos, even though I was wet! How much less than my ninety kilos when I had weighed myself with Gastón in Mendoza!

I hobbled down a corridor and when the nurses opened two doors, there, like a picture, like a surrealist painting, were some of my loved ones, so longed for, so thought about, so dreamt of. They were the most important thing for me, for whom all the suffering had been worthwhile.

Soledad, my mother, my sister Mema, my sister Marti, Pololo, my dear uncle Carlos Algorta, my aunt Elsa, and Beto, my inseparable friend and cousin, as dear to me as all my family. There was also my future mother-in-law, Martita, and her daughter María Martha (Soledad's sister), and Verónica Algorta – a beloved cousin of both mine and Pedro's, who was a Braniff stewardess and had flown from Lima to Santiago. I looked at them one by one, I hugged them and held them, and the happiness that came over me felt incredible! They were part of what I most desired – my family. And in that first contact, I realized that I had returned to life, to my old life, carrying with me a wealth of experience, which I hadn't yet analysed or thought about, but which was with me and needed to be shared with my fellow man.

We went by taxi to the Sheraton San Cristóbal Hotel, at the foot of the hill of the same name. I desperately wanted to see my companions of the mountain again. I missed them and wanted them very much! And I also needed them.

Returning

I found most of them seated, eating and drinking everything that appeared on the table.

I also found Miguel and Jean Pierre, the brothers of Daniel Shaw and Alexis Hounié, who both died on the mountain. I knew them from before and, overcoming their pain, they hugged me in silence, in a long and tight embrace.

There were parents and relatives of others who hadn't returned, but whom I didn't know. I had known their sons, of course, and to this day I am proud of them. And I am grateful to their parents.

I drank some orange juice, thereby beginning the process of securing my long, loose, teeth in their bleeding gums... Vitamin C making an appearance after so long!

Journalists, photographers, and the curious, local and from all around the world, descended on us like a swarm of bees. They surrounded us, photographed us, and thrust their microphones in front of us in order to be able to catch our words.

People I knew, and many I didn't know, came to say hello, almost suffocating me at times, but making me very happy. The reporters wanted to know everything, but for me it was still very private and I didn't want to talk about it; I just wanted to be with my own people, with my loved ones and with my friends from the mountain.

And to think that we had planned to return by train via Buenos Aires, and to call home from there to let everyone know that we were alive! We never imagined such a commotion!

One night in Santiago, some people I didn't know took me, along with Pancho and Gustavo, to eat and drink at a place full of women. I remember Pancho dancing, and Gustavo also, wearing Rueda alpargatas. I remained seated, without the breath to talk, and very weak, and I refused any invitation to dance. I just wanted to leave; what was I doing there among people I didn't know? I wanted to be with my own people. A Chilean took pity on me and took me back to the hotel. And there I found myself totally alone, just like the moment when I lost Bobby, climbing the mountain two months previously. I had continued up without noticing his absence and had found remains of the aircraft, the kitchen or toilets – I don't remember which – and two wheels from the landing gear. I sat there and took in the immensity of the place, and I looked in amazement at the track left by the fuselage, astonished by how it had managed to avoid the black rocks that were lying in wait for it. It was as if someone had guided it. Then I felt panic, a real fear of being alone, and I quickly slid down the slope, sitting on a cushion. I almost crashed into Bobby, who was lying on his back, smoking a cigarette. Later, we arrived back at our 'cottage' and I was overcome by great joy to see my people; my family of the snow. It was my home at the time.

Once I was back at the hotel, I needed to urinate, and the bellboy pointed me to the downstairs toilets. It was very late at night. There was no one in the lobby, it was completely empty. I went slowly downstairs and when I returned I had this long steep staircase to contend with, and I began to climb it. I managed ten steps and then I fell, exhausted, just as on the mountain. Ten steps and my chest was exploding. I was overcome by a strange sense of fear – I was in a hotel, but alone, and no one was coming, despite my calling out in a faint voice. Later, the bellboy helped me to get up to the ground floor, and pointed me to my room, as I didn't know which was mine, and nobody in my family was there. They had gone out and I don't know why I felt, or was, so alone.

In my room, I turned up the air conditioning to maximum, and went to bed, but no sleep came! Later, my brother and my cousin Beto, who were sharing the room, arrived back, and turned down the air conditioning because, according to them, it was icy cold. Once they were asleep, I turned it back up again to its highest setting.

I got up early the next day. I wanted to feel the heat of December and enjoy the colourful surroundings of the hotel. The shower proved to be so powerful that, such was my weakness, it knocked me over, and I couldn't get up, feeling the strong pressure of water over my fallen body. But then my cousin Beto, who was nearby, helped me. I dressed in some trousers, and a T-shirt belonging to my younger sister, which fitted me perfectly, and, looking at myself in the mirror, I no longer saw a chap who was dying, but a resurrected and happy Coche. My mother had brought along a suitcase full of my clothes, but these were several sizes too big for the new package!

Breakfast is always one of the best things about staying in a hotel, but I mainly ate with my eyes, because I would feel full after just a few bites. Half an hour later, I would repeat the process again, and again my small stomach would say "Enough!" And so on, throughout the day. Over the five days that we were in Chile, I gained ten kilos, or two per day.

And we spent those five days strolling through Santiago, enjoying the contact with the people, hearing the horns of the cars that were greeting us, and receiving as gifts anything that we happened to try to buy. The Chileans are very friendly people, as well as brave and courageous. People like Sergio Catalán and family, Commanders Jorge Massa and Carlos García, and Sergio Díaz of the Andean

Rescue Corps, who slept in the fuselage along with my eight companions who were still on the mountain on the night of 22nd December.

On the night of 24th December, Christmas Eve, a Uruguayan living in Santiago volunteered to organize a celebration of family and friends, and to take care of everything. His surname was Fuentes. There were all kinds of delicacies and huge quantities of drink. We toasted those present and those absent, and I felt the presence of the latter in me more than ever. I was raising a glass, rather than dying! Christmas had arrived... accompanied by the gift of a miracle.

On the mountain, we had decided not to mention the necrophagy. Our parents agreed to keep the secret. But although we found the subject tremendously difficult to talk about, we didn't feel so 'guilty' in the strict sense of the word. Also, it had been a profound dedication from one to the other; a covenant of life. But somehow the news sneaked out, and, in a sensationalist weekly tabloid, a headline appeared: **Cannibalism!**

Whoever wrote it didn't understand the difference between necrophagy and cannibalism as described earlier. On this and some other occasions we have been branded as cannibals, which is a conceptual, linguistic, and journalistic error. Unlike cannibalism, necrophagy is not a habit or custom – throughout the centuries it has happened in various circumstances, usually as a necessity for survival.

We decided then to return to Uruguay, and there, in our own country, to tell the world, and above all our compatriots, the truth, and the whole truth. It would be hard, but we would deal with it.

We flew to Uruguay in a LAN plane which, I believe, was provided by President Allende, with an anti-panic crew at the ready to provide reassurance to those passengers who might suffer from the flying, having gone through such a traumatic experience. Most were very nervous. Daniel, Alvarito and Bobby had already returned to Uruguay, and Nando remained in Chile a few more days with his father and his sister. Roy spent several more days recuperating in a clinic.

The arrival in Montevideo was unimaginable. There were thousands of people on the terraces of Carrasco airport, and all along the Avenue of the Americas, waving their arms, greeting us, welcoming us with banners... our people opening their arms to us... We had returned to our beloved Uruguay!

We travelled in two ONDA buses directly to Stella Maris College, in whose gym the press conference would take place. The entire five-kilometre route was lined on both sides of the road with people waiting for us to pass. When we got to the school, the buses were barely able to enter, and even less park, because of the number of people surrounding them. My friend Rolo Saccone managed to get on the bus, and, together, we forged a path through the crowds.

We entered the college via the back of the gym. We waited in the locker room with some of the fathers and some Christian Brothers and took the opportunity to establish the order of appearance of each one of us and the themes to be treated. Dr Jorge Zerbino, Gustavo's father, asked me if I could talk about the topic of the food. I told him "Yes." Others would talk about different things.

But as the minutes passed, I realised that I wouldn't be able to find the words to communicate to the world everything that had happened. Even though we had overcome it, it would still be a taboo subject. I felt that the theme was too big, it was still very intimate for me, and I wouldn't be able to do it.

When we went out to the stage, Pancho sat down next to me. The gym was full, packed with an expectant crowd. I told Pancho that I wouldn't be able to speak, that I didn't have the strength, and to my great relief he replied that he would deal with it. I felt light as a feather.

When I stepped forward, I told the moderator, Daniel Juan, that Pancho would speak on the topic of food, and then I spoke of the cold, the water, the cigarettes, the night-time, and a few other things. I felt stupid that I couldn't face it, but in fact it was the best thing that could have happened.

Pancho found the necessary words, elevated them to a mystical level, and spoke slowly and deliberately, and with much respect. It produced an absolute silence which, seconds later, was broken by the applause of everyone there, who rose to their feet, continuing to applaud.

And that was the end of it! The ordeal of communicating the truth was over. We knew that it would be very hard for everyone, just as it had been for us.

I have always felt gratitude for everyone's understanding, for the understanding of the Uruguayan people, and of the world, but above all for the understanding of the parents of those who died and for their great generosity. Some of them published letters of support in newspapers, or expressed it to us personally, telling us that they were proud that their children were, in some way, living on in us!

Also, the Catholic Church in our country, as well as Pope Paul VI, issued letters celebrating the good news of Christmas.

Returning

I returned to my house in Punta Gorda, from where I had departed seventy-eight days before. I returned to find my dear friends, Sapo Sapriza and Gustavo Pérez, among many others. I returned to the life I had dreamt about, for which we'd done the unimaginable, transformed the impossible into reality. The suffering had stayed up there; now a new life was beginning, one which was giving meaning to what had gone before, and which, projected in the record of my notebook, had given meaning to what was to come.

I went with Pancho several times to visit Gastón's mother, Blanca Jardi de Costemalle. She had lost her husband some years previously, then her younger son Daniel, and now, on the plane, her only remaining son, Gastón. Within a few years, she had lost her entire family. I can't imagine how she could recover after so much pain. It gave her joy to see us, and she always welcomed us with a hug and a smile that showed her humanity and her generosity of spirit. We reminisced together about Gastón and it did us good to talk about him. And she would tell us about how when Gastón would 'go to rugby practice', you would hear glasses, bottles, and ice clinking together inside his backpack. What good times we had! And what good times we would have continued to have! Because if none of it had happened, I would, today, surely be drinking maté with Gastón and many others, instead of writing down these memories. I would know his children and grandchildren and he would know mine. But our story was another, and we can't change that. I guess that my life would have been fairly similar to what it has been, but I would not have that void that the chubby Gastón left in me and several other friends who were saved in this accident. He didn't even have the chance to fight, he left us in the very first moment of the crash. Today his family is reunited in the continuance of their existence.

Today, also, I often recall Vasco Echavarren and Arturo Nogueira; they were badly wounded but I never heard them complain. They were always inside the fuselage, doing what they could, such as locating places on the maps, and always giving intelligent opinions. Swear words were exchanged on occasion, as well as loud laughter. They were courageous, very brave, and endured with courage and faith. They were surrounded by tenderness in their last days, and I vividly remember how some companions fed them and gave them drink up until the last moment.

I have often been asked how my life would have turned out if those seventy-two days hadn't happened. And I answer that I don't know – one cannot know. I do know that what happened in 1972, what I felt and suffered, is a wound which has now healed, but which remains in my memory. And above all, what I will never forget, are the revelations that kindled my life, and which I am compelled to share and explain.

And if there is something I regret, it is not having given more on the mountain, in those seventy-two days of the seventy-two years that I have lived. To have given more, as Numa did.

At the beginning – for the first sixteen days – I was active, although I felt the effects of the altitude; and, accompanied by Bobby Francois, I was even able to hike up the trail made by the fuselage.

After the avalanche, the gangrene in my leg prevented me from walking any more, because the pain and the inactivity gave rise to an increasing physical debilitation. But it made me mentally stronger, and I decided to take control of my despair and anguish, my anxiety and fear. Because that depended on me, even though everything else depended on the others. In the words of Piers Paul Read in *Alive*, I became a 'parasite'. And certainly, the feeling of being dependent on others is not at all pleasant. But with mental toughness I was able to make it less disagreeable, and my friends contributed to that.

I am happy not to have been a parasite. And, what's more, to be someone who gave everything, or almost everything, to save himself and the others.

I endeavoured to stay lucid, primarily for my own good. Then I strived to maintain my self-control in order to restrain anyone who was getting out of line! Because it always concerned me to think what might happen if too many of us were to cross that imaginary line between life and death simultaneously.

I tried, day or night, to raise smiles in the others through humour; and achieving that was very gratifying. We made jokes; sometimes dirty; sometimes very dirty. We would stop when someone warned that Liliana was nearby, but she would ask us to continue, because it made her laugh so much. Laughter was an infallible remedy to defuse tensions and conflicts, and to momentarily forget the reality surrounding us.

I would also think about the Faculty of Agronomy. A strike, lasting a few days, was what had given Daniel, Fito and me the go-ahead to fly to Chile. At the time, I was alternating between studying, and working on the dairy farm in Florida. And I moved from one place to the other by bus or train. It was that part of my existence that had been ruptured by the Andes experience. For all other years, life has smiled on me constantly, and I give continual thanks to God and men, for the closeness that I've had with them, having absorbed their many examples of values that give rise to happiness.

March 1995

In March 1995, on the initiative of Roy Harley, we hired a bus and loaded up the last three rows of seats with huge quantities of prepared foods and drinks. There were twelve of us who left Montevideo, headed towards the Andes, to a place that we only knew through photographs – the tomb of our friends. We arrived at the Sosneado Inn, where we spent the night, and the next day we headed to the banks of the Atuel River, where our horses awaited us. We mounted, and, under the guidance of several local experts, we crossed the river, and in a long single file we started our ascent, passing through high and narrow gorges, and looking at the different colours that certain elements, such as iron, sulphur, and talc give to the walls of that huge mountain.

In the evening, we camped in a valley called El Barroso, and we spent the night there, but not before eating steak sandwiches accompanied by abundant amounts of drink.

The next morning, we started the day ascending the mountain, already very steep, and we crossed over fast-flowing rivers swelled by the meltwater. We were seeing water flow in those places for the first time, since it had been frozen when we were there.

The first snow soon appeared, and our jollity gave way to the silence of the memory of what had happened twenty-three years previously. And then, appearing in the distance, that distinctive geographical place; that horseshoe-shaped valley where we were in 1972. I recognized it right away and, getting closer still, I also recognized, by their shapes, the rocks that had surrounded us during that painful sojourn. Continuing slowly, we passed, to the right, what was still left of the plane's tail. The landscape up there at the top was recognizable, but it was confusing to see it free of snow.

The only thing that could be heard was the panting of the horses and the sound of their hooves on the stones dislodged by other horses.

On which hill had they put the tomb? After having climbed a small rise on foot, it was an incredible experience to find the cross which crowned the grave. We looked at it for hours in silence, each one remembering in his own way. All our friends lay there, and they were also in us, inseparable for ever. I cannot share with you the sensations of being at the grave of my fellow companions, not because it is intimately mine, but because I lack the vocabulary to do so. Please forgive me for that!

We put a bronze plaque at the foot of the cross, and from there we saw the glacier, much lower down, where the fuselage was already trapped by ice. We looked at the new topography, which was now revealed, the same as it always was, but which we weren't familiar with back then because it had been hidden under metres of snow. We scrutinized the headwall which Nando and Roberto had climbed on the last expedition, and it seemed to me that what they did was superhuman.

We put up a few small tents without having been able to find a single metre of ground which was horizontal and had no protruding stones. In the late afternoon, the horses descended back to Barroso to graze, and I found myself helpless and very nervous. Suddenly, the cold of the Andes hit us, and we had to take refuge in the tents where, along with Tintín and Pancho, I couldn't sleep a wink.

During the night, I went out to urinate and I couldn't finish because the cold was immobilizing me. It was an eternal night at the foot of the grave. The experience seemed so distant, and I couldn't imagine how we had managed to be there for seventy-two days.

At times, I felt the same as before, and at times I felt I was just living in the present.

With the passing of the hours I became calm again and I knew that God had returned to be there amongst us as a custodian of the tomb, which could not be on a more impressive altar.

It is comforting to think that, except for the first night of 13th October, nobody else died in the darkness.

I remember gazing at the nights through the oval windows and seeing the stars, one very bright amongst them. I would count them. When there was a full moon I would see the mountain portrayed, and then the moon would disappear for a while until it appeared at the next window. I no longer know how long it took for that change of scene.

My mother was simultaneously observing the same bright star and the same full moon, and she knew that I was also doing it, and vice versa. She did it on the rambla of Punta Gorda, and I did it leaning back inside what had once been an aircraft, now fallen and wrecked in the Andes.

I would continue watching the movement of the moon, like a blind man who has regained his sight, like how a starving man eats; insatiable for life, I had wanted to touch that moon in the same way.

Sometimes some heavily stacked clouds would allow only the highest stars to appear. That life of the clouds would animate the darkness, sometimes lighter, at other times more intense. It was sometimes as if immense shadows would appear to deepen the night.

At times, there was such longing to escape our prison there that we would talk about whether it might be better to be in a prison cell in Montevideo. And we would fantasize about how many years the sentence might be, even considering life imprisonment. We substituted years in prison for days on the mountain, but we didn't know how many more there were to come.

The Valley at Night

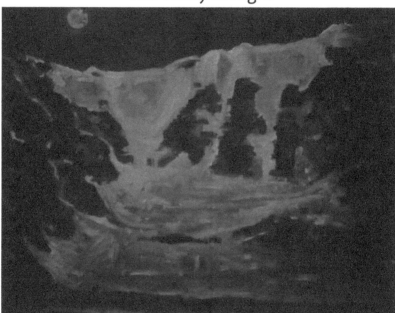

The next morning, on our pilgrimage to the valley, we were eating breakfast, when I heard a noise as if an avalanche was approaching. It was the horses appearing at a gallop. I felt so much joy that it was comparable to the time that the helicopters had appeared. I wanted to leave, I didn't want to stay on that mountain, where looking at that familiar environment weighed heavily on my chest.

My friends could not be in a better place, but I didn't want to be there one minute more.

That was the first time that I returned. But later I went back to visit the site, along with my family, friends, and pilgrims from other countries.

In that tomb lie the bodies of Gastón and my other companions.

It had been twenty-three years from that 13th October, when I had seen him for the last time, to that day when I stood beside his grave. I had survived the mountain and had made my life, and I silently recounted it. He, who did not survive – will he have made another life? When we meet again, he will tell me what today I can only imagine. Until then, Gordo...

This whole story has made me many new friends, who are scattered throughout all corners of the globe. Especially Carlos and Andrés Arismendi of Medellin. We first met by mail, and then they went with us to the site of the accident. Since then, I have felt as though they are brothers, and they even asked me to be the godfather of Marianita, daughter of Andrés.

There is also a fan club with members in many countries – they have a web page called *Re-Viven*, and they are essential contacts for any consultations about this story, including for the sixteen survivors.

1974 saw the appearance of the first official book, *Alive*, which tells the story in a detailed and chronological way, and which became a bestseller. Several documentaries followed, and certain differences began to arise among us, because only a few were chosen to appear in the documentaries, whereas most of us didn't want to appear, and never did. We began what we called our 'prevention machine', presenting a majority source of information, at a time when we thought that it was just a single story. As time passed, we began to understand that there are sixteen true stories of the same fact.

I learned later that the herdsman had been the protagonist in our salvation. And what he did astonishes me. Without knowing us, he gave up hours of his time, perhaps putting aside important things, or not so important but still his own. And for what? For some boys that he didn't know and had only glimpsed across a river... And there we see this humanity arising, this solidarity and salvation, in a simple man; a man of the fields, without great knowledge or culture. But he showed us a heart full of humanity, full of love, because that's what it was, a huge act of love! Forgetting about himself and devoting himself entirely to rescue lives of those that he didn't even know, feeling compassion and pity, and sacrificing his time and his fatigue, just to give a hand to those in need. Relying on his instinct rather than on any knowledge, and carrying out the obligation of a good man; helping, being alert, moving heaven and earth to protect our lives.

Returning

His extraordinary capacity to serve amazes me still today. There is no doubt that I'm here thanks to this chain of efforts that began with the quick actions of that simple and glorious herdsman, who exalts all mankind.

I don't remember having cried in front of anyone in those days, but I was continuously crying inside. What I saw was heartrending, and it tore me apart internally.

To live without hope is almost to die, and that's how I felt during those last days, without dreams, without hope, without future. Crying for the lost life, for the uncompleted projects, for those dear to me to whom I would perhaps never return to embrace. Then I prayed... and it relieved my soul, and that internal force came – I never knew from where – but it came... and as a gift from God, I was filled with peace.

Chapter VIII My reflections

Awareness, choice, and guilt

From my conversations with my therapist, whom I consider to be a wise and humble man, and a man of peace, I've further confirmed and clarified for myself the meaning of life.

The first thing he said after reading the manuscript of this book is, "Don't alter it! Because it is fresh, and authentically yours."

It's the same with the conferences that I give throughout the world, sharing my personal experience of life in the Andes. People have always wanted to instruct me or guide me on how to put them together, how to communicate them, and what vocabulary to use. And I have always refused to become a semi-professional communicator. All I know is how to speak from my soul and address my words to the souls of others. I don't know any other way to do it. Because this story lives in my soul.

The same with these memories of mine. My explanations throughout this book leave my soul and are directed towards the soul of the reader.

I think that I could have sealed this document in a bottle and thrown it into the sea, and if someone someday had found it washed up on a beach, opened it and read this message, I would have been more than satisfied.

The consciousness that we possess must stand at the front of the queue. And for that you must be attentive to its presence.

The truth of what you experience is made real by the conscious state of your mind. From the very first moment on the mountain, I was always aware of what was happening and what I was experiencing...

What has happened? The aircraft has crashed into the mountain! By the time the fuselage has reached the end of its precipitous slide down the snow-covered mountainside, what I see and hear is already real; it is truly happening! I'm immediately aware that my previous life is no more, that I now have a new existence ahead of me.

And I begin to live it at that precise moment. Because I am alive! I have no choice in the matter. It has happened and that is enough!

I'm also aware of not feeling sorry for myself about what happened, but the problem or conflict arises as to what to do about it. The first thing that went through my mind was to flee, but that was impossible.

I chose, like everyone else, to go to the aid of the wounded. Aware of the reality, we did the right thing; what is good, what men must do. And so I helped those who were moaning in their suffering, and I put myself in their place, and I suffered and moaned with them.

It was very difficult to choose what to do! There was no more than comfort and a caress for the wounded, so that they would know that they weren't alone.

The continual great conflict about what choices to make began to enter one's mind: the 'why' and the 'for what'!

And then came the news that the search had been called off, after we had chosen to sit and wait for a rescue that we had assumed would come soon. That made us aware that we were alone, abandoned, and that we should no longer count on anybody but ourselves. Yes, we made this compulsory choice ourselves, and each became aware of the importance of the others for their own survival. We had one another, and there was no-one else. And it was a conscious choice that cleared up a conflict: the hope of a rescue that would come from outside; from an outside which was unconnected to our own efforts.

Later, a new conflict engulfed us, in the form of an avalanche. An avalanche of snow. At that instant, I was completely aware of what was happening. And after trying to escape it, I was left trapped, unable to move. I chose or let myself succumb to the inevitable, to death! There was no longer any choice. And three days later, as the last and only option, we frantically dug a tunnel which took us from the darkness of our tomb into the light.

And that was certainly a choice to continue living, struggling to defend and honour life, despite the very real suffering. Death was the other option which no-one consciously chose.

Up to this point, the pilots of the aircraft were the only ones to blame.

But when we became totally aware that we would have to feed on the bodies of our dead friends, the choice leading to that decision was very tough, cruel, and I even considered it unfair. And even more so when I forced my body to obey the command of my mind.

Several times, in a struggle between the conscious and the unconscious, I considered the other option, which was death.

Although I didn't consider myself guilty of what I decided to do and consequently did, I did in fact feel guilty for a long time, because there had been another option.

I was very mindful to choose life, to honour and respect it as the principal human right, and so I forced myself to do what was necessary to stay alive. I was not guilty, because it was what a man should do in those circumstances, but, nevertheless, I have felt guilty and I apologize to my own conscience.

And over the course of my life to this present day, I have also felt guilty about not having put my conscience first. And I don't apologize for that, but I do regret it.

I've just learnt that guilt is a factor that contributes to breast cancer and it is true! In the autumn of 2013, I developed a malignant tumour on my right breast. They removed the breast and the lymph nodes in my armpit. I also had chemotherapy. But the worst thing was when I went to get the mammogram! I was accompanied by my wife, and pretending to be a supportive husband. Except for the person taking care of us, there was no-one there, and I sat down to wait with Soledad. But the following ten minutes saw the arrival of more than a dozen women who all sat down around me! A nurse came in and yelled: "INCIARTEEEE... José Luís." My heart dropped to the floor with the gaze of all those women fixed on me. I fainted – I couldn't help myself – and I felt guiltier than ever.

On 1st November, after the avalanche, having made our way outside through a hole, and sitting on the snow in a new setting, we were given a new opportunity to face life. The divine presence that I sensed among us showed us the way to peace, which appeared for the first time. And the presence of peace within our ongoing conflict and suffering was not chosen by us.

I think that our God chose us with total awareness so that, in his image and likeness, we would take the steps necessary to lose all fear, to be free and so to arrive at the truth that gives meaning to life and existence.

And from that point on, we were men who made the right choices and who were successful despite choosing the wrong route to get out of the Andes.

My reflections

We chose to do everything to return to the most important thing that man has built: his family. And we did it as a team, because we all wanted the same thing.

Awareness and choice, awareness and choice. Awareness of the truth and choice of the right path. The path of the good, starting with ourselves.

A guilt that I carry with me, or something that I sometimes regret, is not having given more on the mountain. And I take, as an example, Numa, who never tired of being good, and of giving and giving himself.

My therapist taught me that in order to be able to give more, you first have to give to yourself. And I thought this way also, when I used to take pleasure in pouring myself another whiskey, or smoking another cigarette, without knowing that they are unconscious acts, which lead you to choose the wrong path, because both these pleasures put you and your health at risk in the long run.

Today, I try to pay attention to everything that is bad for me, and which therefore hurts those that I love most. And sometimes I let what my subconscious is saying be expressed in a conscious way.

Power and authority

On the mountain, there were two groups with power. One group comprised the three Strauch cousins, who oversaw the food. It was their stewardship of this fundamental resource that granted them the power, and I think that Fito was the authority amongst the three of them. Authority derives from the person and not from a specific resource. Fito was the inventor and through his creativity, forged in the direst circumstances, he was able to share solutions with the rest of us in order to solve the most serious problems. He was generous and gave and gave of himself in the form of his time and energy to help his fellow companions.

The other group with power comprised the expeditionaries, because their willingness to start walking into the unknown gave them the primacy which they they made good use of, which had been granted to them by the rest of us, and which allowed them to enjoy certain privileges.

I think that Parrado had the most authority during and after the ten-day trek. Because once he was saved he had the courage to get into a helicopter to search for us and rescue us, returning to that painful place from which, with indescribable effort, he had managed to escape.

And Canessa was always an authority, which made him a leader. His vocation to serve, his tireless activity, his permanent sacrifice for others, along with his character and temperament, turned him into a leader through the authority that others granted him. And he was also our doctor on the mountain!

It was authority that prevailed over power. Because power is only a circumstance, but it would be orphaned if there were no values to accompany it.

Authority emanates from man and his values placed at the service of his fellow man.

Anguish and fear

I am sure that we all had moments of extreme anguish. I don't think anyone was spared from going through a period of great anxiety, but luckily it didn't overwhelm us all at the same time.

Fear was also present, and I think that it was even more acute in those who had to face some big responsibility, as was the case with the expeditionaries. I imagine that the fear of going out into the unknown, to cross the Andes on foot, was the reason Roberto delayed the sewing of the sleeping bag, broke what had already been done, and was in a continual bad mood. We always had to tolerate his bad moods. The terror that he faced! That was not the case with Nando – he had wanted to leave much earlier. Luckily, he didn't go through with it, because had he done so, the snowfall and the wintry temperatures would have killed them both without any doubt. They left on 12th December, at the appropriate time because from then on it didn't snow anymore.

And Roberto set out despite his fear. Courage is born out of deep fear. Roberto had as deep a fear as I had myself. Courage is to think: 'I'm afraid but this what I have to do. I might as well die walking side-by-side with Nando, rather than die staring at one another in the fuselage.'

I remember with much sadness Numa's death in the arms of Pancho Delgado. 11th December brings back memories of men giving and giving themselves for others. They are images that I cannot forget, and which remind me always that I am also a man in their image and likeness. They are unforgettable examples of what I try to explain about human behaviour.

Wedding Day

On my wedding day, surrounded by the young survivors and by Carlos Páez Vilaró.

It could be said that, in the years following the tragedy, I led a quiet life, forming and raising a family alongside Soledad. The best years were those in which we lived in the countryside, bringing up Josefo, Matole and Maru, my three joys.

I worked like any other resident, chasing after pesos and bank loans like so many others, but above all I enjoyed the pleasure of family life, and being surrounded by friends.

Why didn't I die, why did I survive, and for what?

The truth is that I don't know, but I will try to express what I have thought and meditated about over all these years, again and again...

And I start with the simplest and most straightforward, because I'm delving into issues in which I'm no expert.

Memories of the Andes

I board the plane in Mendoza, and just as I'm about to sit down next to Gastón in the last row, someone else sits there instead. I continue further forward, passing the wings, and sit down next to Menendez on the left side of the plane, on the aisle.

After the crash, in which I am left almost completely unharmed, I see that the section of aircraft that was previously to the rear of me is no longer there; it has been severed just behind me.

The right side of the fuselage is more destroyed because this was the side to which the fuselage was tilted during the slide down the mountainside.

And when everything gets violently thrown forward after the abrupt braking in snow, nothing or nobody crushes me, because there is nothing *behind* me.

Is it that my position was just a lucky place within the lottery of everything that happened? It would seem that it was a matter of chance; some were lucky, others not...

I gave thanks to God for being alive and healthy, without knowing if He had intervened, directing chance and fate; life for some, death for others.

And if God intervened, what criterion did he use to choose who would live and who would die? Even back then, I asked myself, 'For what?'

But this is to enter more difficult and complicated territory. Let's continue down the path of simple and straightforward reasoning.

That first night, I am saved once more. I find Roberto Canessa and, embracing, we give each other human warmth, and are able to see a new dawn on 14th October 1972. I give thanks to God once again for my staying alive, and to Canessa for his warmth.

I can hardly believe that we didn't freeze that night, dressed as we were in light clothes, savagely lashed by a wind- and snow-storm which entered into the fuselage as the guest of honour at this feast of death. Chance and luck stayed with me; with me and Canessa, and I gave thanks just in case God had something to do with it. But there were others, for whom there had been no luck, or God, or anything! Only death. The final point of a short life... within an eternal existence.

Logically, everyone should have died, but something far above us, beyond our comprehension, was guiding what happened. It had already begun to be obvious to us that this was not a case of excess luck, that there was more to it than that... and to complete it all, Nando, whom we all believed to be dead, was slowly returning to life.

My reflections

Our existence was presented to us as a gift, like faith and salvation, and life started to become a substantial novelty for me, where, as the Uruguayan author Tucho Methol Ferré says, one lived out of gratitude, or in gratitude.

Then the inevitable happened, and we were left with nothing to eat. Here it was not a question of good or bad luck, it was not a matter of chance. It was the circumstance of our existence, the life that we had to live, and we could only choose between living and dying. Not even dreaming.

Everyone chose life, to defend it and honour it, and we did what man must do in certain circumstances, to turn a blind eye to the scruples, fear, and taboo with which we had grown up, and to face reality with valour, courage, and a degree of harshness. And I forced my body to do what it had to do, even though it refused. I felt that we had saved ourselves! In every sense of the word salvation.

I think that luck is to chance as life is to existence. Later, chance once again uses its strange logic to choose who lives and who dies in the infamous avalanche that buried us, when we already thought that things couldn't get any worse. It gives us eight more bodies, which indicates to us that this is going to continue, seemingly without end, like existence, which is eternal. Chance repeating itself once more, determining whose life is cut short in this existence, and whose life continues, even in suffering.

For those of us who remained, the pain of the loss of those who left us never, never, surpassed the joy of having had them there, having co-existed, however short their life in this eternal existence. Better to have lived, even for a short time, than never to have lived at all. They left us so much that it was a privilege to have known them and, above all, to have been their friends.

And, quite simply, I was saved from dying in the avalanche because I had changed places with the team captain Marcelo Perez, at his request: sitting facing Fito who, minutes later, would be among the first to be uncovered. So when I had already abandoned myself to death, on my way to meet my father, Fito was able to extract himself, and I followed close behind him.

I returned to this life once more, as a result of luck, perhaps due to the place that I happened to occupy. But I returned to life at its most difficult, even though it deserved to be lived. Perhaps the eight who didn't survive had the better luck in the continuum of existence? I don't know, but I know that they ended the stage of life, and began another stage of existence.

After getting out, the presence of God was evident among us, and, I believe, unanimously so.

From that point on, we gave everything, or almost everything we had, our very best, and what was missing was, without a doubt, added by our friend God, through heroic attitudes and acts full of love, manifested in the behaviour of men.

We made every effort not to leave anything to chance, we wanted to control and plan the final expedition to its smallest detail. We left what we didn't know to God... I don't know if He directs fate, if He chooses this for us or not! But it is true that 'the more I work and the more I do, the more luck I have'. And from then on until the end, a long period in which I was injured and unable to do much, my fellow companions helped me, and took care of me with devotion, love and sacrifice, so that I would keep on clinging to life.

And I reached the end when, stripped of my physical and spiritual strength, exhausted from fighting and suffering, and with the light of hope already lost, I gave up, and I said, 'Enough, no more...!' And I decided that everything would end in two days' time. I was setting a date for the end.

But no! That wouldn't be decided by me. And this time it was not just luck; it was willpower, courage, and the strength in Nando and Roberto's legs: it was God in them and through them. It was the herdsman, who in his great act of generosity of spirit, left everything to help them.

And finally, the courage, the bravery and the heroism of the commanders and the crew of the helicopters, who, like gladiators, fought against nature, against gravity, against their own fears... and rescued us from the mountain! From the place Nando had guided them to!

I feel the presence and strength of God in all of them, without subtracting an iota of merit from the human condition.

Ultimately, maybe all of us become a little like God when we act in His image and likeness. It is what we are, with all the strength of our values and weaknesses.

And so I survived...

And finally, for what did I survive...? To live the life that my existence gave me; and I have certainly lived it to the full!

The only thing that differentiates me from any other human being is the different personal experience, that I lived those seventy-two days in the Andes; I feel that the 'for what' is the chance to share this story with others, to tell them about the God whom I met, and His son, the man. This is something that I want and I need to do in this life, because I have already spent seventy-two years of my existence living it!

Can anyone explain this?

My mother was a staunch Catholic, and we used to go to Santa Rita Church in the Punta Gorda area. I would go with her and sometimes I would take Communion but I didn't want to go to Confession. Why am I going to confess all my sins to this 'playboy', who is a man just like me? I'm going to confess them to God, whom, in addition, I know. He is a different God. He is not the one found in temples. Because God was a man, the most important man. When you pray, you're talking with Him, you are asking Him to 'deliver us from evil'. When you pray for things, it is as if He is talking with you. It calms you. It is something divine that I experienced when I got out from the avalanche. It was there when I got out. Everything was white, and clean. When I emerged from the hole, everything was white and unblemished. I could see neither the fuselage, nor the dirt that we had made, nor the bodies. And you saw your companions emerge from the snow as if they were being reborn.

We already knew that eight had died, because we got out on the third day. Eight dead and nineteen still alive. Three more died later. And sixteen remained. Why are sixteen of us still alive when we should all be dead in the avalanche? Once again? Can anyone explain this?

And when you go out, you feel the presence of Jesus Christ sitting there amongst us. It was the presence of God expressed through man. Because the transformation that immediately occurred was remarkable. And that's where we enter the biggest undertaking of my life, which was to do everything possible to escape the mountains and return to my family.

For the nineteen of us, having spent the most unfair, undeserved, and painful three days of our lives, buried along with the fuselage by an avalanche, preserving our life appeared as the biggest or most important self-struggle that any man could bear. Because there, in the darkness you wondered, 'Why? What did I do to deserve such suffering?'

Once we were out on the third day, I compared it to the resurrection of Jesus.

Sitting on the clean snow, and seeing my fellow companions come out of the excavated hole – that was when I felt the divine presence amongst us. I just felt that it was there and expressed through us.

It was not the God that we meet every Sunday in the parish church. Perhaps our circumstances made me sense Him so differently, so closely, like a friend, as if He were wanting to show us the way to peace and truth. And I could see it in my fellow companions... so I sensed him and, as a Catholic, I call him Jesus Christ. Others give him another name, but I think that it's the same thing. Like the trunk of a tree, which is unique, and there are as many creeds as there are branches from the trunk.

And just as he suffered and was crucified to save us through his sacrifice, I felt that the death of our eight friends had been to save the nineteen, who, like Jesus, rose on the third day. Given the state we were in, so close to death, such a coincidence generated great mysticism, which served as a form of support during those tremendously hard and painful moments. All this allowed us, at that moment, to return to life with hope and confidence, as we had opened our souls to truth and peace, because we, as men, had been made in the image and likeness of God.

And so I knew God's presence, and I think that it certainly exists, and that it is the same for all men of good will.

When I look at the world of today, so troubled, I believe that it is the absence of love that causes so much pain.

I am Catholic, and I believe in God and in men whereby He continues to express Himself through those who have opened their hearts and their souls...

I want to share the truth that was revealed to me then. About what our existence is, and what meaning it has. To be better people, and to love our fellow man as we love ourselves.

Sometimes we achieve it and sometimes not. But we must not fail to try.

Meriting it

This is an extraordinary story about ordinary men; a story of anthropology, man and philosophy, that is to say philosophical anthropology which unites sociology and theology. Sociology, which studies the social interactions of men, and provides data and statistics. And theology, which relates men with God, and reveals values. And this story of ours is based on this. Because if there is one thing I know that gives meaning to life and death, if there is one thing that has been shown to me with total clarity that I want to share, it is this: to achieve the peace that all of us seek, you must travel the path of happiness. And happiness must be merited. It's not free for the asking, it cannot be bought, and it's not something you just encounter.

And to be happy you only need to realize how much more rewarding it is to give than to receive. That is the point. And when you encounter this peace, all your fears disappear, you are no longer afraid, and so you become free.

My reflections

You find yourself in total freedom, and the truth reveals itself to a free being. And what is this truth? The truth to convey is the road towards peace that I've just described. And the truth shows you that what gives meaning to life is this: that during your lifetime you leave something in someone else, and that person also leaves something in you. Living it not just as an observer but being active and involved. And the starting point is to give, to leave something in the other. And, without any doubt, this helped us in our suffering. And that, in short, is the truth of this story.

Chapter IX Thirty years later

Thirty years passed and 2002 arrived; the year in which we got together again with the Uruguayan Air Force at the behest of Colonel Mariano Rodrigo, whose children were studying at Stella Maris College. He organized, at the request of Brigadier Malaquín, a traditional 'asado' barbecue at Boiso Lanza, the Uruguayan Air Force (FAU) headquarters. There were several of us there, along with the Air Force Command of the time. I remember that initially some of us, including me, were strongly pointing the finger of blame at the FAU for what had happened. Later, the atmosphere calmed down, and since then peace has reigned, and some lasting friendships have formed. They recognized that the overconfidence of pilots, along with other factors, were the cause of that terrible human error.

For twenty-nine years, but above all between 13th October and 22nd December every year, it was constantly in my mind: the pain of hunger; the thirst, the cold; the anguish; the smell of the snow and the fuselage; the image of the mountain that trapped us, and the resentment and defiance over what had happened. But time is the best healer, and the best ally to ensure that what's important prevails over lesser things. Everything that I learned and felt about solidarity, courage, and bravery given abundantly – in short, the love which man extends towards his neighbour. And the memory of this behaviour still makes me emotional today. It fills me with pride, the fact of belonging to the brotherhood that arose up there between the living and the dead, who live and will live in me forever, and that's what I wish to convey.

Also, something 'clicked' in 2002, not only in me but also in others in the group... thirty years had already gone by. Time cures and heals all wounds, and the need arose to share and recount our story. It's what differentiates me from normal earth-dwellers – those seventy-two days lived in the Andes. So I began to give lectures or conferences, together with Álvaro Mangino, and we discovered that it did us good to talk about it. And it was a more than pleasant surprise when we realized that we were also doing good to those who were listening to us; and this last aspect made me continue, and be among those who started the Fundación Viven, along with Diego Canessa, Gastón's godson.

Fundación Viven has the mission to go to the rescue of people whose life is a daily fight for survival, and its main programme is the donation of organs, emulating our covenant of life in the mountain. After several campaigns, the Uruguayan Parliament voted in a law by which everyone is a donor from birth.

Today, the Foundation has a travelling museum, which is itself a work of art, and transmits all the values that gave us life on the mountain. It is available for travel throughout the world, to share many human values far and wide.

The extraordinary

When we were on the mountain, we had no inkling of the commotion and the array of journalists, cameras, and the curious that would descend on us from all over the world after our rescue.

We believed that we had been given up for dead in October, and that no-one would still remember the Uruguayan plane that had crashed in the Andes with forty-five people on board.

Even in Los Maitenes, the first place where the rescue helicopter landed, it came as a big surprise to see so many people with cameras and tape-recorders, speaking in different languages. Who were they, and what were they all doing there?

I didn't understand why our survival was so important to the world, nor why they were filming me so much and taking so many pictures of me. Not until I realized that the important thing, the extraordinary thing, is the story itself, experienced and told by ordinary living people. How could I have survived seventy-two days? Over and above having to use our friends for food – the principal means for our survival – there was also the 'why', which was just as decisive. And the 'why' continues to arouse great interest in people across the world. Books, documentaries, feature films, magazines, radio interviews and conferences continue to take survivors to different corners of the world. It is of interest because our story encapsulates the story of all mankind and the meaning of his existence.

Ours is a timeless story, which can be located in any time or place.

It still surprises me – when I give a talk to 200 people or more – to see the interest in their faces and their body language; their need to know, to understand what we experienced, to share what we suffered. And when I finish, when the standing ovation has died down, they come over and hug me, and once again I feel comforted for what I experienced, and I feel the love of these people, whom up there, I reiterate, we never imagined we would welcome. And it surprises me, because it hasn't diminished over the years; on the contrary, the interest has increased. And I feel that I must give thanks from the bottom of my heart for all these displays of love and interest.

Giving a talk

My imagined wake

Up there on the mountain, time passed very slowly. Sometimes the days were longer and sometimes shorter. When the sun was out, I even came to appreciate and admire the nature that surrounded and imprisoned us. I saw and felt the beauty, and it moved me.

But if there was no sun, or when night came, it was eternal. The darkness was sometimes deeper, sometimes lighter, but the hours passed as if they were frozen by the cold, as if the height mattered to them, as if they needed more oxygen to make progress. It was another world.

And so I had more time to think and to imagine...

I thought a lot about my mother and about Soledad, to whom I would already be dead, and how they would be suffering. Or perhaps they would still retain hope, because, I presumed, no part of the aircraft had been found. And it distressed me greatly, both to think about them and to be powerless to tell them that I was still alive!

I would imagine the people who would pass through my house, to be with them and mourn with them... and I made lists of people...

When I returned home, I asked about my 'imagined wake'. I was very surprised to find out who had gone to the house almost daily, simply to provide company; the appearance of people I never imagined, and for whom, since then, I have had a special love and affection, even though I don't see them.

I also found out that my mother and Soledad had never lost hope. And although they suffered indescribably, they relied on the lack of confirmation about what had happened. They had absolutely nothing to tell them that I had died. I was also surprised to hear them tell me all the possible excuses they would use to continue hoping and to justify my absence.

'Our Children'

In August 1973, ten months after the accident, the mothers of our friends who died on the mountain, with much valour and courage, transformed their pain into something very positive for the children of our country. They founded the Biblioteca Nuestros Hijos (Our Children's Library) in memory of their deceased family members. And to this day, already forty-eight years on, this library continues its work of contributing to education and culture. Our friends must be proud of this undertaking, which was done with so much strength, valour, and faith.

Today, the brothers and sisters of our friends have taken the next step, giving the library a thriving and modern profile, with new technologies.

I have had a good relationship with the families of those who died; with some more than with others, as happens in life. It has not been easy to overcome this blow, neither for them nor for us. But some parents approached us from the very first moment, questioning us, anxious to know all about their children, and embracing us with affection. For others, it has been more difficult, and perhaps for us also. I think that they ask themselves why we returned, and not their children... a question that I continue to ask myself, and I get no response.

Anyway, I have some much-loved friends, such as Álvaro Pérez del Castillo, the brother of our rugby captain Marcelo, with whom I maintain a deep lifelong friendship, which I value and am grateful for, and which, I feel, did not wane after what happened. I remember vividly his welcoming embrace when we met, charged with emotion and affection. There, I also embraced Ines, Gastón's girlfriend. Another hug full of sadness.

My fellow companions

There have always been differences amongst us survivors, sometimes relating to self-promotion. As the years passed, these differences have become exacerbated. And it even seems that someone else accompanied Canessa and Parrado in the crossing of the Andes... and I don't mean God!

There are also differences of another nature, which sadly have never been overcome.

I contend that up there, we all underwent the therapy that we failed to undergo as a group once we returned home. Thirteen of us met, once only, with a psychiatrist and a psychologist in order do group therapy, because of the possible post-traumatic shock. We had decided to wait for them to speak first, and it looked as if the doctors were thinking the same thing. And after ten minutes of total silence on both sides, Gustavo Zerbino said that it was boring, and we left. That's not to say that we haven't visited a psychologist in our lives, but if so, it is for reasons almost certainly not attributable to the Andes. Seventy-two days is a long time! Even when you're having fun...

After the rescue, when I got back to civilization with my camera in hand, the roll of film that had captured scenes of our lives on the mountain was no longer inside. A few years later, those unique photos, which we had taken ourselves, appeared throughout the world, distributed commercially by an international image agency. Already, earthly life was taking hold, and values were changing.

Life is a natural right, the primary human right, and, as such, it has a counterpart, which is the obligation that it entails. That's why defending life, honouring it, and meriting it, was what led us to comply with that obligation in different ways. Up there, we always tried to keep hope alive, and this only weakened when faced with the death of a friend. And what anguish that caused, weighing heavy on our hearts!

Thirty years later

Every 22nd December, on the anniversary of the rescue, we get together. Although we have hardly ever managed to have everyone present – for different reasons, there is usually someone who cannot attend. Today, together with children and grandchildren, there are around 140 of us. If the mountains are eternal, man is also eternal in the ongoing extension of his existence.

When I am asked what my fellow survivors are for me today, I say that they are my friends. They were companions for seventy-two days in 1972 and today they are my friends, they are not brothers. What has united the sixteen of us, I think, is what gave us life and what we carry within us: our friends who died and whose bodies we used for food. That is the common denominator that sixteen men have held throughout their lives: carrying inside us those companions who could not return to give happiness to their families.

That is what unites us. I see those who did not return in each of us, and that's why I love them, as well as for other things. But I believe that the common denominator that unites us most in this life is to carry those who could not return and to try to live with dignity in their memory; nothing more.

We were together for seventy-two special days. It is a spiritual community of fellow companions, and as such we have our differences and arguments, some very difficult. But we know each other very deeply, very intimately, and we forgive everything. Some are more friends than others, and some we don't see too often, but when we do, we feel that we are bonded forever.

We never forget our dead friends. We don't forget our living friends. We don't forget what we experienced.

We have gone more than once to the site of the accident, with friends or in a group. My children have also gone. We have carried flowers to the grave. Every time we go, we draw a special energy from the place, and we return more enriched.

I've come to live with these memories that are so painful. Time has already healed the open wounds. But the images are still in my memory, perhaps already lifeless, but full of blood and pain, and always full of courage, devotion, and heroism.

Describing them sincerely for this book has been an immense effort for me.

In 2002, I stopped all professional and business activities, and coinciding with my initial experience of becoming a presenter of the Andes story – on 22nd May of that same year – I started attending the Cruz del Sur painting workshop, at the request of my friend Adolfo Albanell. There, I found an exceptional group directed by art master Sergio Viera, and the alma mater of the workshop, his wife Lilian. Since that time, I have been going every Wednesday without fail to learn how to paint in oils, and to enjoy the company of my fellow students. This activity must be one of the best possible therapies. All the paintings in this book were painted in this studio (www.tallercruzdelsur.com).

My art master and friend, Sergio Viera, taught me everything I know, and took me from the figurative to the abstract, without which I would not have realised much.

I learnt that a good painting is dependent on a good drawing, and so I spent many a class drawing.

I have put on several exhibitions in my country, both individually and collectively, with my dear workshop colleagues.

Sergio has written the foreword in all my catalogues, and there is one that I particularly want to share:

Using rich lessons from the old master Cezanne, that a painting must comply with certain rules that make for a 'good form', Inciarte poses his own expressive problem. Focused on this, he gives flight to his unconscious to give us images, which range from strong contrasts to others that are more poetic, of the countryside that he knows so well, and of urban landscapes.

His work is highlighted by a sensitive but firm line and by a spontaneous and sensual shading, which hints at the open and vital man that is Coche Inciarte.

In this way, he paints as he lives, for the moment, and without unnecessary complications, joining these qualities with an intuitive and sensitive spirit. Perhaps because his experience has allowed him to appreciate the unique moment that is now, and to enjoy deeply the experience of living.

However, it is likely that this is already known, because I suspect that there are men who carry this burden of wisdom, and for whom the abstruse and the affected is off-limits, and who already know that the important things are usually the simplest.

Sergio Viera

Epilogue

In the first days of January 1973, people from the Uruguayan Air Force, the Andean Rescue Corps, and the Chilean Air Force, went with priest and mountaineer Iván Caviedes to our mountain.

They brought together the bodies of those who had fallen from the tail of the plane, which had remained a thousand meters above the fuselage, scattered at the place of impact, and the bodies that had been around us, and they made a grave in which to bury them all together; an effort that lasted a week.

The priest Caviedes (who died some time later in a mountaineering accident) officiated at a Mass.

The Uruguayan Air Force was represented by Colonel Crossa, who supervised operations over the week that he stayed there, and who finally set fire to the fuselage. Later, he told me that in that week he had changed his way of being and thinking and that, when he came back down, he felt a better man. Perhaps our friend God was still up there.

The tomb is located on a hill on the side of the Valley of Tears. It is simple and is crowned by a cross that emerges erect every year, after the thaw. On that altar lie my friends.

While that was taking place, we were in Uruguay, where we were caught up in our new life in the company of our family and friends, happy to be alive and breathing.

Yes, God helped us up there, but He did it through the men who were with me for seventy-two days on that mountain where no life can exist – neither animal, nor plant, nor human.

The mountain was not our enemy; it has always been there. Nor did we want to invade it, but we found ourselves there through human error. We protected ourselves from the extremes of nature and, with God's help, we finally achieved our survival.

There was no question of revenge for us, because we hadn't fought against man as in a war. It was quite the opposite.

And it is then that the human condition prevailed in its highest understanding, vindicating man, and "helping man to endure by lifting his heart, by reminding him of the courage and honour and hope and pride and compassion and pity and sacrifice which have been the glory of his past," as William Faulkner said in his Nobel prize acceptance speech, 1950.

I have told my story and I have tried to explain myself – no easy task.

The mountains are eternal, and will continue to be there, perhaps for many centuries.

The Tomb in the Valley of Tears

Man's life is ephemeral, but it leads to eternity in another way. It is in our descendants, our children, grandchildren, and great grandchildren, that continuity is assured. Our genes, capabilities, and skills carry who we were and who we are into the future in some way. And so man will endure on Earth...

I know that I will continue in this world, through my offspring, who are my most precious legacy.

Technology, one of mankind's great advances, already shows us the future.

Ultrasound of my granddaughter

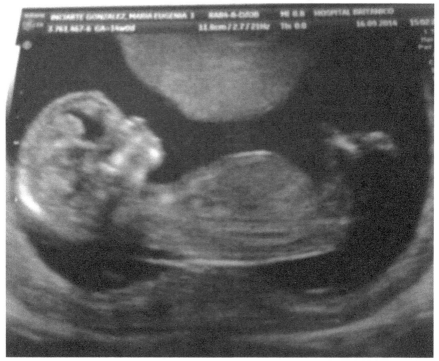

And I wonder, dear Gastón, what it was that remained for me to do in this life in which I exist.

I planted a tree on the dairy farm before travelling to Chile.

Then I got married and had three children.

Perhaps it just remained for me to write a book about my distant memories, and to give my explanations about the human condition; and you and the readers will say whether it has been worthwhile.

Until we meet again!

A big hug from your unconditional friend.

COCHE

PS. *My family today:*

I am grateful to...

Facundo Ponce de León, Pablo Vierci, Mireya Soriano Lagarmilla, María Marta González Mullin, Pablo Gelsi, Irene Arrarte, María Moratorio, Raquel Nogueira, Marti Inciarte, Mercedes Inciarte, María Balsa, José Ferrandiz, Vinicius López Terrone, Xerach García, Gonzalo Aemilius, Carlos and Andrés Arismendi Montoya, María Eugenia Inciarte (my daughter), Soledad González Mullin (my wife), Julián Ubiría and Leroy Gutiérrez.

To John Guiver for giving me a voice in English.

And finally, to my surviving friends who gave life to this book and to those who remained in the mountains, who will always, always be in my memory.

Each one of them knows why I am so grateful.

José Luis 'Coche' Inciarte was born in Montevideo in 1948. He has a degree in agronomy from the Universidad de la Republic.

Over his working life he dedicated himself to Dairy Production and became a director of the National Association of Milk Producers of Uruguay.

After a long and successful career, he retired from his business activities in order to give talks about his experience as one of the Andes survivors, to take painting classes, and to enjoy his family, especially in his role as a grandfather.

John Guiver was born in 1955 and lives in Saffron Walden, England. His professional career has been in the area of Artificial Intelligence research and development with Microsoft and other high-tech companies.

A long-term personal interest in the Andes story has led him to Uruguay, Argentina, and Chile, where he has met with many of the people who were caught up in the tragedy. He has previously translated the memoir of Coche's fellow survivor Pedro Algorta, and is currently writing a book giving a wider perspective on the story, due to be published in 2022.

Lightning Source UK Ltd.
Milton Keynes UK
UKHW020405080421
381596UK00007B/93